Point to Reading™
The Bible

Matthew 28:20 in Action

Henry Skinner-Larsen

Point to Reading Books
Lockhart, Texas
www.pointtoreading.com

Also by Henry Skinner-Larsen

Point to Reading:
Hope for the Future Through the Love of Reading

Apuntar a la Lectura de la Biblia
(Spanish version of *Point to Reading the Bible*)

Point to Reading Books
Lockhart, Texas
www.pointtoreading.com

ISBN-13: 978-0991585205 (Point to Reading Books)
ISBN-10: 0991585208

Web sites offered as citations and/or sources for information
on any subject may have changed or been removed at any time.

Cover design by Amariah
Point to Reading™ and PTR™ are trademarks of the
Point to Reading concept and Henry Skinner-Larsen.

"Humility is not thinking less of ourselves;

it is thinking of ourselves less."

On a church wall in Tanzania, Africa

"These words, which I am commanding you today,
shall be on your heart.
You shall teach them diligently to your sons,
and shall talk of them when you sit in your house
and when you walk by the way
and when you lie down
and when you rise up."
Deuteronomy 6:6-7

Dedication

Respectfully, I thank our heavenly Father who gave us His Word. I thank my parents for reading to me when I was young; the people who taught me to read; and those who encouraged my love of reading. In particular, I thank those who encouraged me to read the Bible. I remember distinctly the moment when the veil lifted and suddenly I recognized of whom John was speaking when he wrote,

"In the beginning was the Word..."

With the desire that all people may learn to read well and come to appreciate the wisdom and beauty of the Bible, I dedicate *Point to Reading the Bible.* I have written this book in the hope that you, who read these words, will be moved to offer your time to share your love of the Bible with another. Whether you mentor your child, a neighbor or a friend, this is a meaningful way to fulfill the Great Commission.

In the spirit of Matthew 28:20, may we offer others a way to make disciples through a Bible-reading relationship, teaching them to observe all that our Lord has commanded us to do.

CONTENTS

Introduction

WHAT IS THE POINT TO THIS BOOK?

You might think this book is about why you should read the Bible. It is not. Books on Bible-reading are plentiful. What you are about to read may surprise and, hopefully, encourage you into action. You will discover an easy way anyone can fulfill two essentials of our faith. These essentials are foundational to what it means to be a Christian. I think you will agree—doing these two practices will have a profound impact on your joy and understanding. Through them you will produce much fruit in your life. Is this not what we all want, so that one day we will hear the words, *"Well done good and faithful servant..enter into the joy of your master."*

> ### *So Jesus was saying to those Jews who had believed him, "If you continue in My word, then you are disciples of Mine;*
> ### *And you will know the truth, and the truth will set you free."* John 8:31-32

What will set us free? The truth. And where will we find it? In the words of Jesus. Are they only the ones in red letters, or just what we find in the New Testament? If the Bible is the inspired word of God, wouldn't that mean the whole Bible? I realized recently that Jesus never once quoted the New Testament. And since Jesus regularly quoted from the Old Testament, dare we overlook one bit of what he considered the truth?

Obedience before Understanding

What does it mean to *"continue in My word"*? In any master/student relationship, the student needs to obey the word (the commands or teaching) of his master. Is Jesus not telling us—to know the truth, we must obey his word, proving we are his disciples? But, if we do not know his word, and do not obey what his word tells us to do, how can we expect to know the truth? Listen—obey—understand. Many do the opposite. They want to understand first, and then choose to obey (which makes a mockery of obedience). Obedience must come before understanding.

The foundations of the faith highlighted in this book are <u>Bible-reading</u> and <u>Discipleship</u>. Before you throw this book back on the shelf, afraid it will be boring and tedious because you've already heard those sermons, I hope you will give it a chance. This is a short book that you can finish in a couple hours. Keep in mind that the benefit doesn't come from just reading the words, but when you do them.

> ***But prove yourselves doers of the word, and not merely hearers who delude themselves.*** James 1:22

The point to reading the Bible is to read it and to do what it says. This book is about *becoming doers of the word*. And what you are going to learn and then do is very easy—easy to understand and easy to do. I am excited to tell you that for those of us who may never go to a foreign country, our mission field can be in our homes and our community.

If you have struggled with trying to read the Bible, you will learn an easy and enjoyable way to become the Bible reader you previously only wished you could be. And you will discover it through another foundation of our faith—Relationship. The simple act of reading the Bible with another brings transformation to you and others in ways that will delight you. In addition, you will discover a fun way to step out in obedience to the Great Commission, to go and make disciples. Imagine fulfilling these two foundations of the faith by reading the Bible with someone—building new and better relationships, with our Father and with others.

> ***Beloved, let us love one another, for love is from God; and everyone who loves is born of God and knows God.*** 1 John 4:7

What a perfect way to grow our relationship with God—to read His Word, and then become doers of the Word. And imagine the joy of the Lord when we read the Bible with someone, encouraging another into a deeper relationship with our heavenly Father, the source of love.

> ***"By this all men will know that you are My disciples, if you have love for one another."*** John 13:35

Chapter One

BEGINNING WITH THE FOUNDATION

It's all about relationship.

Whether the topic is religion, business, or family, this is a well-known remark. We may agree, but do we fully recognize how much relationship matters? How does relationship impact faith or family? What is the measure of a quality relationship? And what does relationship have to do with reading the Bible?

Many mistakenly believe that relationship is something we do as part of our faith, business, or family. Some think quality relationships improve our interactions with others. On the contrary, outside of relationship, there is no faith, business or family. The relationship is the faith; it is the business; it is the family.

> ### Relationship is not the means to a thing.
> ### It is the thing.

We confuse ourselves when we mistake physical closeness for relationship. Would you describe sitting next to someone on the bus as being in a relationship? Does the act of walking into a church bring a person into faith? Is there no lonelier place than in a crowd of strangers?

The tragedy of false relationship is played out daily in marriages which end in divorce. After the smoke clears from the destruction of the family, an all too common remark is this: *"The person I thought I knew all these years is a complete stranger to me now."* Suicide is one of the leading causes of death for teenagers in America. How much does a lack of true relationship contribute to someone feeling so alone that the only solution is to die? I have read that newborns need to be touched, suggesting that if human touch were totally withheld from a baby, within a short period of time it would die. Besides the obvious needs of food, water and air, it may be that the greatest human need is relationship.

Can a pretend relationship bring the benefits of a real relationship? Is the nature of relationship so mysterious, so difficult to understand? Or is relationship so obvious, so simple that even a child can do it? This book is about building deeper relationships while reading the Bible together.

What is reading without relationship?

As the author of **Point to Reading**, I have spent years encouraging parents to build a relationship with their children through reading. The essential rules I use to understand reading, learning and comprehension are the common sense rules of relationship. To build effective reading skills (while building the love of reading) we need to ask this question: Does the way we teach something strengthen or hurt the relationship? My #1 *PTR* rule: *If any practice hurts relationship—don't do it.*

How's your own relationship with reading? Many adults avoid reading because it was taught as an unpleasant task to perform instead of a fun adventure. Performance is the opposite or enemy of relationship. Think back to first grade when you were called on to stand and read out loud in front of all the other kids in your class. That's performance, and it's scary. Any wonder so many kids (and adults) hate reading?

Educators are coming to the realization that our children are losing their love of reading in the first grade. Once a child decides that "reading is dumb" and "I'm not good at it", he gives up. Education for the purpose of creating a love of learning may be over. The only hope is that an adult mentor will step in to rescue that child's love of reading and learning.

It's all about relationship. Relationship between a child and learning. It's about relationship between a student and a teacher. Pretending to be in a relationship is certainly not the same as being in a relationship. In sports, the team which truly works in relationship *as a team* will beat a disconnected group of superstars. Where there is no relationship, or false relationship, everyone and everything suffers.

Somewhere along the road to modern education, we convinced ourselves that workbooks, TV shows, and computer programs could replace real people for teaching our children to read. We traded the human teacher for an entertaining machine. We gave up the difficulty of relationship for the false god of efficient mass production. Yes, we turn out students who know how to read—but don't like to do it—and who also understand little of what they are reading.

Relationship is what gives everything its meaning. It's the relationship between letters which forms words. The relationship between the words creates the meaning in our sentences. The relationships between the people are the heart of our stories. Without relationship and meaning, words would be nothing more than black marks on a piece of paper.

By removing relationship from how we teach reading, we have made it so unpleasant that few bother reading anything that isn't demanded for their jobs. Under these circumstances and for other reasons, few read the Bible. And they have no idea what they are missing.

The all-time best-seller which few have read

Reading the Bible is about having a relationship with the author. The painful truth is many believers know a handful of verses, but have never read the Bible. Many think that knowing a few stories and how the book ends are all they need for a relationship with the God who wrote it.

If all believers (whether they go to church or not) were regular Bible readers, then this book might not be necessary. I don't want people to buy **Point to Reading the Bible** and put it on the shelf. I want you to read it. Then I want you to use what you have read.

> ***What good is it to own a Bible and not read it?***
> ***What use is it if we read it, but don't follow it?***

> *But He answered and said, "It is written, 'Man shall not live on bread alone, but on every word that proceeds out of the mouth of God.'"* Matt 4:4

Some believe this country's problems are caused by **too much Bible**. I believe our personal, family and business problems are due to **not enough Bible.** Removed from schools, and public places, it's missing even in some churches. Why? Because few people read it anymore.

With so many distractions, few find the time. On top of that, we've mistakenly believed that Sunday school and listening to sermons can replace reading it ourselves. Yet, if the followers of Christ don't know and live his Word, what hope is there for the revival our church and country desperately need?

Can we ignore this any longer?

This book focuses on two essential practices of Christian life:

1. Regular reading and meditation on Scripture
2. Discipleship as described in Matthew 28:18-20

According to published studies and my own discussions with hundreds of church-going Christians, these two areas of practice are practically ignored. Some may disagree as to whether these are commanded. Would you agree these practices at least borderline on being commanded, and should be more than mere suggestions to follow if we feel like it?

And yet we (churches—believers and elders) go on year after year pretending not to notice the elephant in the room—this neglect of these two practices. Tragically, we fear there is nothing we can do about it, so we ignore it, hoping the problem will go away.

Practice #1. Bible Reading We have all heard at least one sermon (if not many) on the value and importance of daily Bible reading. To those who do it, they nod their heads in agreement, grateful for the blessing of Scripture in their lives. To those who don't, sermons on the practice of Bible reading are little more than a source of guilt. For many it can be one more boring sermon that is forgotten by lunch.

Years back, right after I had finished reading the Bible, I was curious about how much other people read the Bible. I surveyed several hundred people I knew to be serious believers, asking them two questions:

1. *Do you read your Bible every day?*
2. *Have you read the whole Bible, every chapter and verse?*

At first I was shocked by the answers, because I was asking people I knew to be visible and dedicated members in their church. Some were deacons or Sunday school teachers. Consistently, the answer was "no" to both questions. Many would look at the ground, saying they know they should, but "just can't find the time." For some it was, "I try, but it makes me sleepy." Not one person ever told me he thought it was unnecessary or a waste of time. Most were clearly uncomfortable, aware that *they should*. They believed it to be important, but somehow couldn't get past the obstacles that have prevented them from doing it.

Practice #2. The Great Commission I remember a sermon from the Baptist church in our small Texas town titled ***The Great Omission***. The pastor clearly did not believe Jesus' words should be considered a suggestion. *"Go and make disciples..."* He was encouraging us to make it our commission, not our omission.

I've discussed Bible-reading and discipleship with pastors and elders. They recognize the problem—these practices are absent from the lives of their church members. Trying to do something about it, they focus on the areas they can have an immediate impact—sermons and Sunday school. I appreciate sermons and listen to great teachers as often as I am able. But listening is passive, and it is not the same as reading the Word myself. Instead of encouraging Bible reading, pastors may inadvertently enable people to just "let the pastor tell them what the Bible says." Believing there is no answer to this lack of Bible reading and discipleship, we've given up looking for a solution. The elephant is still in the room, and ignoring it won't make it go away.

I have yet to meet a believer who said Bible-reading and discipleship are unnecessary. But, ***do they think they are important***? What does our non-Bible-reading behavior say about our beliefs? We pay our electric bill, and rent or mortgage. Those are important. When Jesus taught on being known by our fruit, wasn't he saying: *Regardless of what we say, our actions reveal what is truly important to us.*

Is reading the Bible important? Consider these reasons for reading it; then you decide whether it is worth the sacrifice of your time.

1. We learn who the Lord is and what he's done for his people.

An abundance of Bible stories tells us his people were commanded to do such and such—so they'd remember the Lord and what he has done. Is it fair to say that many of the problems of the Israelites happened because they forgot God? Judges 2:10-11 warns us,

> *And there arose another generation after them who did not know the Lord or the work that he had done for them. And the people of Israel did what was evil in the sight of the Lord and served the Baals.*

There are numerous times that Scripture instructs us to teach our children so that this failure doesn't occur. In the Judges 2 example, the generation which crossed the wilderness after leaving Egypt—people who witnessed the miracles and heard the voice of the Lord—failed to pass on what they knew to the next generations. Their children forgot God.

2. The Bible is the rulebook for this game we call life.

Like it or not, the Creator created the game, the field we play on, and all the people in the game. On top of that, he wrote all the rules by which the game is played. If you don't like his rules, then you can... Oops, there is no other game. Yes, I know there are people who will tell us there are lots of choices for how we can live our lives. They want us to believe there are different games to play. The God of Abraham, Isaac and Jacob says there is one game and he created it. If someone wants to believe there is another game, they better hope they are right. If they are wrong, they just might have to spend eternity sitting on the bench.

Following this game metaphor, do you think it would be a good idea to learn the rules and follow them? Do you think it might be helpful to practice your skills for the game, so when you get your chance at bat or to run with the ball that you will be able to "run the race and win the prize"?

3. Can we consider that Scripture all but commands it?

Some people argue that nowhere are we commanded to read it. In a literal sense, that is true. The Bible also does not command us to breathe, but few would argue against whether breathing is needed. Is God's Word not the breath for our souls? Are we truly disciples of Jesus if we do not study what he said and how he lived? There are dozens of verses in support of Bible reading. A number of them will be highlighted in this book. The longest chapter in the Bible is Psalm 119 which extols the beauty and perfection of the Lord's instructions. A central verse for this book is Matthew 28:18-20, the Great Commission. How can a believer disciple another, "teaching them to observe all that I have commanded you", if he doesn't know what the Bible says? Since Jesus clearly commanded that we "go therefore and make disciples", would it be fair to say we can consider ourselves commanded to learn the "all" that we are supposed to teach others to "observe"?

4. Reading the Bible builds our relationship with the Lord.

This is one reason that is not so obvious. **Relationship**. How many times have you heard this remark?

Our faith is about relationship, not rules.

Adam walked and talked with God in the garden. Abraham was called a friend of God. David was a man after God's own heart. They are our role models—people who had a personal relationship with the Lord. We are encouraged to do the same. Today, how does it look to walk with the Lord—which means to be *in relationship* with him?

If someone who loves you sends you a letter, do you read it? If you love him or her, I'll bet you might read it more than once. As believers we repeat John 3:16, about how he loves us so much he sent his only son to die for us. *And then we can't bother to read the rest of his letter to us*? Really?

How many times have you read or heard that the Lord wants to be our God, and we his people? <u>*Relationship*</u>. We are encouraged to pray, to speak directly to him. <u>*Relationship*</u>. Reading the Bible is a way to spend time with him and grow that relationship.

5. Reading the Bible is a way to hear his voice.

I have favorite authors I have listened to in public, or on the radio and CD's. I know their voices so well that when I read their books, I hear their voices in my mind as I read the words. It's as if they are personally reading the sentences to me. The Bible is His words. When we read Scripture, He speaks to us and we come to know His voice.

"Now then, if you will indeed obey My voice and keep My covenant, then you shall be my own possession among all the peoples, for all the earth is Mine; and you shall be to Me a kingdom of priests and a holy nation." Exodus 19:5-6

"My sheep hear My voice, and I know them; and they follow Me; and I give eternal life to them, and they will never perish; and no one will snatch them out of My hand." John 10:27-28

6. The Bible is an invaluable tool for our sanctification.

This may be the most difficult reason to accept. Few people enjoy when someone points out their failings. When we read the Bible, we get to see our own bad behavior in the story of others. That can be pretty hard to handle. Unless you think the Bible stories are talking about somebody else, then sincere study of Scripture can be downright painful. Real change is difficult. But, God wants to change us for the better.

For those whom the Lord loves He disciplines,
And He scourges every son whom He receives.   Heb 12:6

There is no blame for not reading the Bible. Avoiding it might seem less painful. But, there is no avoiding the consequences of our own bad behavior. Is ignorance of the law a good defense in court? Will ignorance of God's laws insulate us from the consequences of our bad decisions? Gravity hurts when I fall and hit the ground. As much as I dislike hitting the ground, life without gravity would be far worse. And so it is with what the Lord wants to teach us. Isn't it better to learn the truth and change than to keep making the same mistakes, year after year?

I want to unveil something else about reading the Bible for our sanctification. We believe that God is personal and alive. We believe He desires to have a one-to-one relationship with us. We believe we can hear His voice when reading Scripture. So, here's my point. When we hear His voice and obey, as in Exodus 19:5; when we hear His voice and follow him, as in John 10:27; then, there are wonderful blessings to be received. Reading the Bible can be like sitting with that best friend who will tell us something difficult to hear, but that we desperately need to hear. In Isaiah 9:6, we are told one of his names is Counselor. Our God offers the kind of advice which will be life-changing if we will accept it and change.

7. The more you read it the better it gets.

Good movies or books can be enjoyed once. A great movie or book improves each time you experience it. You catch things you didn't notice the first time, reaching a greater depth of meaning, as your appreciation of the wisdom and beauty grows. You may be nodding your head in agreement. Yet, many will not get past their difficulties with reading

Scripture to appreciate what the rest of us are raving about. It is just that something wonderful happens when we enter into a relationship with the Creator of the universe through his Word. The better we get to know him, the better the relationship gets.

Hearing people talk about a movie or book they love is boring compared to watching or reading it yourself. The best descriptions of love pale in comparison to experiencing it. Though listening to sermons or Bible teachers is good, it is still someone's interpretation. Allow yourself to hear His voice directly and build a relationship that lasts forever.

8. Be a Berean.

A friend recently told me, "Henry, don't just listen to Bible teachers; make sure you read it yourself." The Bereans were held up as an example for us to follow. (Acts 17:11) Every teaching they heard they tested against Scripture. But they had to know the Bible to do that. Someday we all must give an account of what we did. If I follow incorrect teaching, the consequence will be mine. If I crash my car, it will do no good to blame someone else who told me to turn when I shouldn't have. There's a story of a couple who drove off a bridge while following the instructions from their GPS device. Ignoring the signs, they drove around the barricades just because the computer voice said to. If we believe the Bible is the ultimate road map, then we must learn to read it ourselves.

9. Scripture is our sword and our shield.

There are numerous references to Scripture being a sword. Unfortunately, many believers go into spiritual battle without their sword. Without practice, they don't even know how to use it. How does one learn to use a sword? He must pick it up and practice with it. In time he will become strong and skilled with it.

When Jesus was tempted by Satan in the desert, how did he respond? He met every challenge with a verse out of Scripture. He didn't call out to angels to rescue him. He instead fought with the most powerful weapon at his disposal—the Word of God.

Aren't we to follow Jesus and walk as he walked? One thing we know about him—he knew Scripture. And he used it "for doctrine (teaching), for reproof, for correction, for instruction in righteousness." 2 Tim 3:16

In the desert, before Jesus had chosen even one disciple, he was showing you and me how we are to do battle when we are faced with temptation. But, if we are to be effective in battle, we must pick up the sword and practice with it. We must become skilled, and through our actions teach others to do the same.

For the word of God is living and active and sharper than any two-edged sword, and piercing as far as the division of soul and spirit, of both joints and marrow, and able to judge the thoughts and intentions of the heart. Hebrews 4:12

It's about actually doing it.

Some think this book is for people who don't read the Bible. Nothing could be further from the truth. Aren't there already thousands of books written on the power, beauty, and value of Scripture? Books that explain why we should read it; books about why we should disciple others. Judging from results (fruit), something is missing.

PTRTB is not about **why** you should read the Bible or **why** you should disciple someone. It's about actually doing it. It's about leading people past what stops them from reading the Bible and discipling others—through relationship. It's about how you can easily step into obedience of the Great Commission. In your hands is a way to read the Bible *and* fulfill the Great Commission—*both at the same time.*

It is a wonderful gift to encourage people to step into a growing relationship with the Father who loves them. Will you allow another year to go by, not experiencing the joy of fulfilling the Great Commission in a simple, yet meaningful way? Today is a good day to get started.

Today if you hear His voice, do not harden your hearts as when they provoked Me, as in the day of trial in the wilderness. Hebrews 3:7-8

Chapter Two

HAVE YOU READ THE BIBLE LATELY?

"Behold, days are coming," declares the Lord God, "when I will send a famine on the land, not a famine for bread or a thirst for water, but rather for hearing the words of the Lord. People will stagger from sea to sea and from the north even to the east; they will go to and fro to seek the word of the Lord, but they will not find it." Amos 8:11-12

What will it take to bring about revival in America?

Imagine an America where Christians read the Bible—all of it. Picture our churches full of people with a mature understanding of Scripture. Consider the impact of older/mature believers spending time building relationships with younger/new believers and family members, reading the Bible with them and discipling them in the faith.

But, we know this is not happening in the church today. Recent studies show that few church goers have read the whole Bible, and Bible readership continues to decline.[1] [2] [3] The Great Commission—making disciples—is talked about but few will do it. We have ministries for youth, singles, marrieds and seniors, to build fellowship. Done with good intentions, these ministries result in segregation, not integration. We say discipleship and the Bible are important, but what we do says otherwise.

With more than a quarter million churches, it's estimated that over 70% of Americans claim to be Christians. Yet, studies show church goers have the same problems with bad behavior as those who don't claim to be believers. How are we to be salt and light to the world? We hear calls for revival from pulpits and radio programs. And yet, if every American went to church, *what kind of revival will we have if we don't read the Bible?*

Can Bible reading bring revival?

The story of King Josiah offers insight into one of the lowest points in the history of the Southern Kingdom of Judah. The Book of the Law had been forgotten for years, as Israel and Judah descended into every form of rebellion and despicable practice learned from its neighbors.

2 Kings 22:8, 10-11 *"Then Hilkiah the high priest said to Shaphan the scribe, 'I have found the book of the law in the house of the Lord.' And Hilkiah gave the book to Shaphan who read it." "Moreover, Shaphan the scribe told the king, saying, 'Hilkiah the priest has given me a book.' And Shaphan read it in the presence of the king. When the king heard the words of the book of the law, he tore his clothes."*

This portrays a turning point in Judean history. But, King Josiah did not stop there, as we see in 2 Chronicles 34:30-33. He acted decisively.

*"The king went up to the house of the Lord and all the men of Judah, the inhabitants of Jerusalem, the priests, the Levites and all the people, from the greatest to the least; and **he read in their hearing all the words of the book of the covenant** which was found in the house of the Lord. Then the king stood in his place and made a covenant before the Lord to walk after the Lord, and to keep His commandments and His testimonies and His statutes with all his heart and all his soul, to perform the words of the covenant written in this book. Moreover, he made all who were present in Jerusalem and Benjamin to stand with him. So the inhabitants of Jerusalem **did according to the covenant of God**, the God of their fathers. Josiah removed all the abominations from all the lands belonging to the sons of Israel, and made all who were present in Israel to serve the Lord their God. Throughout his lifetime they did not turn from following the Lord God of their fathers."*

What does revival look like?

Revival involves a change in behavior--*REPENTANCE*. The book of Jonah offers the story of Ninevah as an example. If Nineveh had not repented, exhibiting new behavior, the city would have been destroyed. It is not enough to say, "I believe". Our behavior must change. An argument might be made that Bible reading is evidence of a change in behavior. Can it be both the cause and the result (or fruit) of revival?

What do you believe?

➢ How much effect could reading the Bible have in our churches, our homes, and our schools?

➢ Would our children and youth benefit from having an older person—a mentor—to guide and encourage them?

➢ If people willingly spend time in the Word, won't that tend to increase their ability to disciple others, in addition to making a positive impact on their own lives?

What this book addresses and intends to change is the fact that few Bible-believing Christians have read the whole Word of God. Is this a minor point of faith? Is Bible-reading just a nice thing to do? Or is it food and water for a follower of Christ?

Is it enough to go to Sunday school or listen to a sermon? Would your body be satisfied if you fed it once or twice a week? Years back, when I read the Bible from cover to cover for the first time, I came to enjoy discussing what I was learning with others. In Sunday school, I thought it odd how only a few out of a large class would ask questions or offer any comments. It was like high school where hardly anyone had read their homework. The teacher would do all the talking because nobody had anything to say. In the beginning, I was surprised by how little people knew about this Bible they claimed to love. When I'd mention a story, they often had no idea what I was talking about.

Should we be surprised? I knew little about the Bible...until I read it. I have also met people who do read the Bible. It is obvious. You can tell because they are familiar with the stories and enjoy discussing them.

Are we to read Scripture just so we can know what it says? Not hardly. In addition to being our guide for correct living, the Bible commands us to disciple/teach others. And yet few Christians disciple anyone the way Matthew 28:20 describes—even though we know we should.

What can we do to change this?

I grew up in a house that had a Bible in every room, but nobody read them. Some churches are full of Bibles, yet few pick them up. There are even churches which have none. We are told the Bible is the #1 all-time best-selling book. And yet, surveys say few have read it. Why is this?

Some may argue with the statement "few have read it". Most church-going Americans have read something from the Bible. Even non-believers or people of other religious beliefs know John 3:16 or Genesis 1:1. Many believers know a favorite psalm or Bible story. But, do they really know the Bible? Should we be concerned by this lack of Bible literacy?

I've spoken with many who agree with everything you have just read. They just don't know what to do about it. In their minds, this problem seems impossible to solve. Too big. Never been done before. Yet, if we are going to get a different result, we must do something different. ***Point to Reading the Bible*** is an answer that will work... if we will apply it.

A Turning Point in Education and Learning

For the first time in history, every bit of recorded knowledge is available in seconds to anyone with internet access. Science, art, current events—pick a subject and you can have the facts and opinions of great minds and experts to study as deeply as you wish. We have entered an era of unimaginable possibility. To enjoy this infinite abundance, all one must do is read. And yet, a large majority of adults never built a love of reading and learning. We are like people in a restaurant full of food who starve because they don't want to or know how to eat.

What is the point to reading?

Why do we learn to read? Isn't it to enjoy the stories we find in books, and hopefully to become smarter? Why is enjoyment important for understanding? People generally like what they are good at, and become good at what they like. Though this is a simple concept, it is foundational to someone ever becoming an avid reader. *A person will do something if he enjoys doing it. Doing it for a long time is how he can become good at it.*

Why we don't like to read.

Few love to read, and some read poorly. There are three reasons why people don't enjoy reading:
1. They do not know how to read.
2. They are not good at it, so it is not fun.
3. Something happened to make reading unpleasant.

To get people to read, they need to become good at it. It helps when they enjoy the process of becoming a reader so they won't quit. The principles for how to build the love of reading are covered in **Point to Reading**. This book in your hands applies those same principles which we can use to build the love of reading the Bible.

Problems with reading the Bible

The Bible is not easy to read. Some of the books, for example Paul's letters, are difficult and can be hard for even a good reader to understand. When reading is too hard, people often give up. If a person is going to be a reader of the Bible, he must *"get over the hump"* of difficulty. With regular practice and guidance, the Bible becomes much easier to understand.

> *People tend to like what they are good at, and get good at what they like.*

There are some unique challenges to Bible reading. The stories happened thousands of years ago, so the names and places are strange to us. It can be very difficult to understand what the stories mean when they involve customs and lifestyles so completely foreign to modern living. In addition, the weirdness of the times and places promotes disassociation, preventing us from seeing how these people and stories are like us.

Truth be told, some parts of the Bible are more interesting than others. I attempted many times to read the Bible on my own. I often got through Genesis and Exodus, but if the book of Leviticus didn't trip me up, Numbers would get me every time. I tried starting with the New Testament book of Matthew, but got ambushed by the "begots". I even attempted some of the Prophets like Isaiah and Ezekiel and quickly became frustrated, having no idea what they were talking about.

On top of these problems, there is the *process of sanctification*. God's word was given to change us, not entertain us. Instead of a fun book for light diversion, we are confronted with death, destruction and the general human condition. The Bible is the Lord's instruction manual which one could say is designed to show us four things: (1) who He is; (2) that we aren't Him; (3) what He has done to bring us into intimate relationship with Him; and (4) what He requires of us for that relationship to grow.

For those of us who would admit a desire to be the center of the universe, those are difficult lessons. The message of Matthew 22:37-39 can be pretty hard to accept—that I am to *"love the Lord your God with all your heart, and with all your soul, and with all your mind..." plus "love your neighbor as yourself"*— when my favorite person in the whole world is **ME**.

The fact of the matter

It is amazing, from a certain point of view, that anyone reads the Bible. Don't take my word for this. According to studies by organizations like the Barna Group and others, many professing Christians do not read the Bible. You may not be surprised by the answers I got when I personally surveyed hundreds of church-going, Bible-carrying people about their Bible-reading habit, but I was shocked. I wasn't asking non-believers or people who never go to church. These were people who faithfully go to church and yet had never developed the habit and joy of regular Bible reading.

Why is this a problem?

With the slide in moral and ethical behavior over the past 50 years, has there ever been a greater need for the Truth of God? If a person does not read the Bible regularly and does not know what it says, is an hour of Sunday School and a forty-minute sermon each week enough *"for teaching, for reproof, for correction, for training in righteousness; that the man of God may be adequate, equipped for every good work"*? (2Tim 3:16-17) What we see happening today should convince us that something is missing. What better time to heed this message to Joshua, when he was placed in leadership of the Israelites prior to entering the Promised Land. Note the conditional statement: **THEN** he would be prosperous and have success, by meditating on the book of the law and doing all that is written in it.

"This book of the law shall not depart from your mouth, but you shall meditate on it day and night, so that you may be careful to do according to all that is written in it; for then you will make your way prosperous, and then you will have success." Josh 1:8

What is *Point to Reading*?

My first book, **Point to Reading: Hope for the Future Through the Love of Reading**™4, was written to show parents how they can build the love of reading and learning in their children. *PTR*™ addresses the problem of declining reading ability in America by focusing on basic learning principles. Through a one-to-one relationship, *PTR* makes reading fun and easy. Understanding and enjoyment become the result. It is important to prepare kids for life by building the love of reading in them before they face embarrassment and failure in school.

The principles of *PTR* are used in this book. These principles are common sense, yet somehow get overlooked. The first *PTR* is a helpful resource for a complete understanding of the ideas and practices that are the core of this book. But, it isn't mandatory. Just grab a Bible and follow the simple instructions in this book. All you will be doing is reading and discussing the stories with another. What you need is someone to read with you, whether a family member, a friend across the street, or a member of your church. It may even be someone who is not a member of any church, but is willing to read the Bible with you.

PTR: an easy way to help another become a Bible reader

By following the Biblical model of one-to-one discipleship, *PTR* may be the easiest way to help another learn to read and understand the Bible. Why does *Point to Reading* work so well?

1. People learn to read faster one-on-one with a coach than in a group. Like the immersion method of learning a foreign language, the love of reading and the skill of comprehension are gained quickly.
2. You, who already love the Bible, are perfect for the job. You have the desire for your friend or child to succeed. Your commitment is very important, so that he will not give up. Also, he trusts and wants to learn from you.
3. Your knowledge of the Bible opens the door for your friend to understand what it means. *"So faith comes from hearing, and hearing by the word of Christ."* Rom 10:17
4. You set an example to follow with your own Bible-reading habit.
5. The *PTR* way of one-to-one discipleship is in agreement with Matthew 28:20, *"teaching them to observe all I commanded"*.

Do I have to be a Bible expert to do this?

Not at all. The Spirit of God is our expert and our teacher. Through the simple act of reading the Bible with another, God's voice is heard. Yes, anyone can do this but who will? Will it be the 90% who haven't read the Bible? Or will it be someone who loves the Bible and is committed to serving the Lord? Jesus said *"The harvest is plentiful but the workers are few."* When I tell people about this book, many congratulate me and wish me great success. Do they think a book will somehow make people want to read the Bible? Do I love someone enough to *"lay down my* life" for him, by sacrificing some of my time? We can fulfill the Great Commission by doing something we already enjoy—by simply reading the Bible with another. For this to work, all we must do is love the Lord and love others as ourselves. If we are willing to do that, the rest is easy.

A Word of Encouragement

The end of a book—the last words—are the essence of the story. Jesus' last words were about discipleship and spreading "the Word". Check out these verses found in Malachi, the last book of the Old Testament.

> 3:16 ***Then those who feared the Lord spoke to one another, and the Lord gave attention and heard it, and a book of remembrance was written before Him for those who fear the Lord and who esteem His name.***
> 3:18 ***So you will again distinguish between the righteous and the wicked, between one who serves God and one who does not serve Him.***

Let us be of those who *"spoke to one another"*, being remembered as *"one who serves God"*.

---

1   http://www.religionnews.com/2013/04/04/poll-americans-love-the-bible-but-dont-read-it-much/
2   https://www.barna.org/barna-update/culture/664-the-state-of-the-bible-6-trends-for-2014#.VmhbN4-cEb4
3   http://www.christianitytoday.com/gleanings/2012/september/80-of-churchgoers-dont-read-bible-daily-lifeway-survey.html
4 *Point to Reading* ©copyright 2013 by HSL; Point to Reading Books

Chapter Three

THE MOST IMPORTANT REASON OF ALL

There are many ways a person can learn to read. There are also many ways a person can learn what the Bible says and means. Some methods, simply looking at results, prove to be more effective than others. But, we must be careful we don't make the mistake of believing that one way is as good as another. As followers of Jesus, it's best to copy the example He set out for how we are to live and act. To know and understand Jesus' example for guiding our paths, we read the Bible. As James made clear in chapter 1, verse 22:

But prove yourselves doers of the word,
and not merely hearers who delude themselves.

Obedience to the Lord's commands

Assuming you already agree with the importance of obedience, I won't go into a long argument with an abundance of verses to convince you of the need to obey what our Lord commands us to do.

In addition, I am not suggesting the Bible commands us to teach our friends to read, though we are commanded to meditate daily on the Word of God. What Matthew 28:20 does tell us is that we are to teach them "*to observe all that I commanded you...*"

One simple way to fulfill the Great Commission is to help others to read and understand the Bible. In addition to being able to read and understand the Word of God on their own, someday they will also be able to pass along the joy of reading the Bible to another.

I have no greater joy than this, to hear
of my children walking in the truth. 3 John, verse 4

Can we teach others to observe/obey the Lord's commands if we haven't read and understood the Bible? That might be difficult. Obediently spending some time every day in the Word is one way to make this possible. If you are willing, you are ready to help another. Must a person know everything the Bible says to be able to teach it to another? Not if you let Scripture and His Spirit do the work. When you read the Bible with another, isn't it God who is teaching him...along with you?

Is the Great Commission a command?

When Jesus in Matthew 28:18-20 told his disciples to "go and make disciples...teaching them to observe all that I commanded you", was this a command? It was certainly a command to the eleven. In verse 18 Jesus tells them "All authority has been given to me..." Is authority needed for a suggestion? No, authority is what elevates a suggestion to a command. I believe it is therefore safe to consider His words a command.

Was this command (to make disciples and teach) for those eleven disciples present that day, and them alone? Or is it for anyone who becomes a disciple of Jesus? Since the eleven were commanded to teach new disciples "to observe all that I commanded you", wouldn't the Great Commission be included as one of those commands to observe?

I ask this for two important reasons. First, to refute the idea that "making disciples" is optional. Some say, *"That's not my gifting."* The eleven disciples had different gifts. Yet all were told to disciple. Second, to refute the idea that only seminary trained people should teach.

> *Now as they observed the confidence of Peter and John and understood that they were uneducated and untrained men, they were amazed, and began to recognize them as having been with Jesus.* Acts 4:13

This is not to suggest that there is something wrong with education or training. This simply means we must not hold up education and training as necessary conditions for someone to obey Jesus' words in Matthew 28. When Jesus gave his command to make disciples, he based the command on his authority to do so. The authority to obey and do went along with that command. Based on Jesus' authority, his disciples therefore had the authority *in his name* to make disciples and teach them. If you are his disciple, do you not also have that authority? Look at Acts 4:18-20:

> *And when they had summoned them, they commanded them not to speak or teach at all in the name of Jesus. But Peter*

and John answered and said to them, "Whether it is right in the sight of God to give heed to you rather than to God, you be the judge; for we cannot stop speaking about what we have seen or heard."

What is Legacy?

A legacy is something of value passed down from one generation to the next. It can be physically valuable, as in land or financial wealth. It can also be knowledge. One of the most valuable legacies is an example of the correct way to live. In Deut 6, the Lord commanded Israel through Moses to teach their children of the Lord's ways. If a father teaches his children while they grow up, they will have their father's example for how to teach their own children. Children copy what they see their parents do. By following the example of his father, a son knows it is his duty to teach his own children about the Lord and what He has done for us.

As long as each generation of children learns from their parents, and then teaches their own children, the passing down of knowledge remains unbroken. Should a father fail to teach his children, the chain is broken in that family and knowledge of the Lord can be lost. One of the saddest passages in the Bible is Judges 2, verses 7-11. Joshua and the elders, who crossed the desert wilderness with Moses, had all died.

> 10 *And all that generation also were gathered to their fathers; and there arose another generation after them who did not know the LORD, nor yet the work which He had done for Israel.*

Something prevented the teachings of the Lord from being passed down to a new generation which, therefore, did not know the Lord.

> 11 *Then the sons of Israel did evil in the sight of the LORD, and served the Baals...*

The Lord's message to his disciples in Matthew 28 was to make disciples and teach them, so they can make their own disciples and keep the message alive. Our Lord created us to build legacies. A way to be obedient to Matthew 28 is to teach another by reading the Bible with him. Once that is done, the "disciple" can now fulfill the same command to disciple another. This is the core of legacy.

I think we can be confident that all disciples are to speak the words of Jesus and to teach others to observe (obey) all of his commands. This next part is about a particular benefit that comes with reading and discussing the Bible. That benefit is greater understanding. Let's take a moment to discuss the nature of learning—how people learn and what we can do to become better learners.

THE MOST IMPORTANT REASON OF ALL

Have you ever wondered why Jesus gave us the Great Commission? We have examined the concept of legacy—making sure the knowledge of the Lord is passed down to the next generation. Though it's true that we are to disciple to spread the message of the gospel, could it be the Lord wants us to teach so that we ourselves learn his Word at a deeper level?

There is a common belief that a person must become an expert FIRST before becoming a teacher. If that were true, it would seem that few would be able to obey Matt 28:20, except after many years of study. In this section, we'll examine an idea of learning and teaching that may change what you understand about learning. It may seem backwards compared to "how we've always done it".

Teaching to learn—versus—Learning to teach.

This simple concept—this change in the way we do learning—will have a profound impact on how both a student and teacher learns. I encourage you to take the time to understand this part of the book. Not only will it supply an important reason for reading the Bible with someone the PTR way; this concept can transform how you learn (and teach) in any other area. At the end of this section, there will be an assignment for you.

What most believe about "learning"

Ask people how they learn and most will say they learn by reading or listening to/watching a teacher. This belief is based on the idea that if we gather enough information, eventually we will understand. It defines learning as filling a cup—you just keep pouring into the cup until it is full.

Others will mention learning from experience, or the School of Hard Knocks. Though experience and consequences are a valuable source of information, neither guarantee a person will learn from them. I've met plenty of people who make the same mistakes over and over, refusing to learn from them. Let's investigate a different view of learning.

How learning actually happens

What is true learning? Is it simply the gathering of information? Or must that information somehow change (transform) us to be able to say we have truly learned? In John 8:32, Jesus tells us that knowing the truth will make us free. What must happen for *information* to become *transformation*?

Have you ever "taught" something to a child, and after finishing your explanation, asked the question, "*Do you understand?*" And what does he say almost every time? "*Uh, huh.*" If you then ask him to explain to you what he understands, what does he say?

"I understand it; I just can't explain it."

Hearing that answer, what do you immediately know? He doesn't understand it, of course. So what do we do? We "tell" him again. We think that if we repeat the answer enough times, he will understand. In school, we fill our kids with information. Then we make them regurgitate the answers on multiple choice tests. But, if we ask them to explain it in their own words, we generally get a blank stare.

Some say the ability to explain something is the *proof* a person understands it. Though this may sound backwards, in reality it is the *act of explaining* which brings the understanding. Think carefully about this. One belief says that "learning is all about what you take in." In contrast, "true learning is all about what you give out."

Memorizing facts versus true learning

This is certainly different compared to how we learned in school. But, then I would ask you: *How much do you remember from what you spent time "learning" in high school?* In most cases we sat passively listening to what a teacher told us. We read textbooks and memorized facts. If this had been done differently, might we have gotten better results?

Connecting the dots

True learning happens in relationship. When we take new ideas and integrate them with old (previously known) information, and then explain (share) this new understanding to another, we build new knowledge. People often refer to this experience as "connecting the dots". It's not that we learn something, and then are able to explain it. It's the opposite. The act of discussing the information creates the learning.

Imagine being asked to explain something you are studying. You think you understand it. It made sense when you read or heard it. You agreed with what the teacher was saying. But the moment you try to put it into your own words, it gets all jumbled up. It's like waking from an amazing dream and being unable to explain what the dream was about. This has happened to me plenty. I catch myself wanting to say:

"I understand it; I just can't explain it."

For the person who is willing to go through the discomfort of discussing something new with another, the pay-off is huge. It is during that act of explaining that we increase our understanding. I am sure you have heard this expression: *The teacher learns more than his students.* In Acts 20:35, Paul reminds the elders in Ephesus of Jesus' words:

"It is more blessed to give than to receive."

There is blessing in receiving, but Jesus says the giver gets the greater blessing. And when the gift being given is wisdom and understanding, the giver gets even more wisdom and understanding. Why not apply this to learning.

Telling a story or joke the first time can be difficult. Tell it many times and it keeps getting easier. Why? Is it because you memorized the story? Or is it because you just "know it"? Consider the difference between singing a song you've known since childhood, and a song you just heard for the first time. We have to sing a song a bunch of times before we will know it. I can go into just about any crowd and start singing a famous hymn, and everyone will be singing it along with me. We know when we know something. We can explain it. We can sing it.

How does this learning and memory thing work?

When explaining and discussing, we must put our thinking caps on to "prove our point". That takes more effort than passively listening to a new idea and saying, "I understand". When we passively listen, the idea or information belongs to someone else. "*This is what so-and-so believes.*" To explain an idea, we must take ownership of the new idea. This concept of ownership is key to long term memory and true learning. Can we keep (or learn) something we do not own?

How do we get to remember a good joke? By telling it to someone else. To do that, one must take ownership of the joke. People then refer to it as "your joke". When you discuss an idea with someone, whether they agree or disagree, they will call it "your idea". We must take a risk to connect ourselves to that idea. That idea then becomes part of us. Passive acceptance is like a cup being filled with information. Actual ownership comes through doing the mental exercise necessary for the idea to transform us.

I believe it is through the act of teaching (sharing our gift with) others that information becomes transformation. Consider the metaphor of the Jordan River versus the Dead Sea. The Jordan receives what it is given and passes it along **(trans)**, bringing life to all it touches. The Dead Sea on the other hand keeps **(in)** all it receives, passing nothing along. Would you rather be *in*formed or ***trans***formed?

Long term versus short term memory

Memory studies suggest as much as 90% of short term memory is lost within 24 hours. Considering all that happens in a single day, that is probably a good thing. There is plenty in my life I wish I could forget; but I want to remember the important things. An effective key to saving the important ideas in long term memory is discussion, or sharing the idea with another.

Knowing how to learn is a majorly important skill. America spends billions to help our kids learn. Parents fret when their children struggle with learning. The knowledge for how we can transform learning and understanding is available, if we will use it.

Did you know the Bible gives clear guidance regarding what must happen for learning to occur?

God's ways often seem backwards to us

How many times does Jesus say the least will be the greatest, that the weak will be strong, or that a leader must be a servant? We are reminded that the Lord's ways are not our ways. It's also true about learning. We must teach others if we want to really understand. Consider what Paul says in Romans 10:8-10.

> *But what does it say? The word is near you, in your mouth and in your heart (that is the word of faith we proclaim); because, if you confess with your mouth that Jesus is Lord and believe in your heart that God raised him from the dead, you will be saved. For with the heart one believes and is justified, and with the mouth one confesses and is saved.*

It is not enough that we believe in our hearts; we must also confess it. We must tell someone what we believe. The two are linked in a special way. A person can hear something and believe it in his mind. But something very important happens when we tell another what we believe to be true. Let's take a look at what Jesus tells us in the parable of the talents in Matthew 25. I suggest you take a moment to read the whole story from verse 14 through 30.

On the surface we have the story of three servants entrusted with their master's property. While the master is away, two of them work with the talents given to them, returning double to their master when he returns. To both of them, the master said, *"Well done, good and faithful slave; you were faithful with a few things, I will put you in charge of many things; enter into the joy of your master."* But the one referred to as the wicked, lazy slave decided to do nothing but bury the talent his master gave him. Things did not go too well for him.

What does this story have to do with learning? The answer is found in what God considers a talent. Gold and silver were measured in talents, and the story refers to the talent as money when the master told the wicked slave he should have invested it with bankers. To a human, this "kind" of talent would be a treasure; but what would God consider a treasure? One clue can be found in Matthew 6:19-21:

"Do not lay up for yourselves treasures upon earth, where moth and rust destroy, and where thieves break in and steal. But lay up for yourselves treasures in heaven, where neither moth nor rust destroys, and where thieves do not break in or steal; for where your treasure is, there will your heart be also."

What treasures does the Lord offer of great value? One answer is the gifts of His Spirit. And in His Word we are encouraged to search out something worth more than gold—wisdom and understanding.

How blessed is the man who finds wisdom, and the man who gains understanding. For its profit is better than the profit of silver, and its gain than fine gold. Proverbs 3:13, 14

What are we to do with the gift of the talents our Master left with us? Should we bury it, keeping it to ourselves, until his return? Or should we multiply it, returning more to him than he gave us? Considering the reward for the two who multiplied their talents, the answer is quite clear.

How does a person multiply a gift from the Master?

We multiply a gift of the Spirit by sharing it with others—by giving it away. When we teach someone something, we offer a precious gift—the gift of knowledge. And when we teach someone to observe everything the Lord commanded, we offer wisdom and understanding which is better than silver or gold.

Notice what happens to the servant who does not multiply his talent (his gift). Verse 28 says, *"Therefore take away the talent from him, and give it to the one who has the ten talents. For to everyone who has shall more be given, and he shall have an abundance."* Not only does the wicked servant have his gift taken from him, but the obedient servant who multiplied his talents was given more. This reflects what was said in verses 21 and 23:

"You were faithful with a few things; I will put you in charge of many things..."

When, as followers of Jesus, we are obedient to the Great Commission by teaching another all that the Lord has commanded us in his Word, we accept the gift given to us and multiply it. The one who is taught receives a blessing. And yet, the one who teaches (who has been faithful with his gift or talent) is rewarded by being given even more. Just as the Lord tells us there is a greater blessing in giving than receiving, the one who gives will also receive. In the case of wisdom and understanding, when offering wisdom and understanding to another, the blessing is more wisdom and understanding for the teacher. To paraphrase the sentences from verses 21 and 23, when we are faithful to give away the wisdom and understanding we have been given, we will be given more wisdom and understanding. In light of this, review verse 29, which previously might have been difficult to understand.

> *"For to everyone who has* (**multiplied his gifts/talents—** notation added) *shall more be given, and he shall have an abundance; but from the one who does not have, even what he does have shall be taken away."*

Let's consider the connection between short term/long term memory and the Parable of the Talents? When we are given a gift of knowledge, it goes into short term memory. By sharing that knowledge with another, not only do we get to keep the knowledge (in long term memory), we are given even more understanding. It is through the act of teaching or sharing (**confessing with our mouths**) what we have been given as understanding (**that we believe in our hearts**)—this is what saves our memories and understanding.

The greater blessing goes to the giver

Though both the teacher and the student are blessed, it is the teacher who receives the greater blessing. In the parable, the faithful slave is blessed because he multiplied his talents. The wicked slave loses what is given to him. At some point, every disciple is brought to Matthew 28 and is given the command to *"go and make disciples"*. If the disciple obeys by teaching (giving to another) what was given to him, he will receive the blessing of being given more.

When do we know someone is truly learning?

It is when the student begins teaching another. Jesus tells us we will be known by our fruit. The visible fruit of learning is the act of sharing the gift with another. When do we begin to really learn something? It is the moment we teach it to another. This is our Lord's message in Matthew 28. He wants us to get wisdom and understanding, and we do that by giving the gift we have been given to another.

Here's the assignment mentioned earlier

Would you like proof? It is tempting to believe you understand this idea about learning. I encourage you to test it. Find someone today to share what you have just read. Does this thought cross your mind? *"I understand it; I just can't explain it."* If necessary, take the book and read it to them. Explain it the best you know how. The first time it may be a struggle to remember the details. The more times you explain it, the clearer it will become in your mind and the more confidently you will explain it. This will stimulate new thinking and new behavior in your life. You get to truly learn what you have just read—by giving it to another.

Discussion—a core principle of the Bible

By reading and discussing, verse by verse, with another, we not only plant the seed of wisdom in another, we increase our own. Whenever two come together in the Word, there is always another present—the Holy Spirit, the giver of all wisdom and understanding.

> Matthew 10:20 *"For it is not you who speak, but it is the Spirit of your Father who speaks in you."*

When we read and discuss the words of Scripture with another, we are not speaking our own words but literally those of our Father. Is this not a real way to experience His Spirit moving through us? What a privilege, if we will step out in obedience to disciple another by reading and sharing His Words. We share so many things, like a favorite restaurant or movie. We do it because we want to share something that is important to us. Is there anything more important than the Word of God? Is there any better way to show love to others than to share that with them? Is this not the most important reason of all?

Summary:

Christians have a duty to disciple others. Building a relationship while reading the Bible is an effective means of discipleship. *Reading and discussing with them* builds the habit of Bible reading—in them and us. The most important reason may be that once we step into obedience to the Great Commission, then we (both mentor and student) get to be transformed by the information, learning at a deeper level.

1. For people to become readers, they must become good at reading. To become good at it, people must enjoy doing it, **especially during the time they are building the habit**. The mentor's knowledge and commitment will help the student get through the difficult days in the beginning.

2. Learning happens when student and mentor discuss what the Bible verses and stories mean. Transform. Don't just inform.

3. Make a commitment to your own true learning. When you discover something meaningful, find someone to share what you have learned. Do it that day. Otherwise you risk losing it.

4. Both the student and mentor will be blessed by the obedience of the mentor to teach the student.

5. Legacy is the gift of knowledge of the Lord, passed down from generation to generation.

Share the love of reading the Bible...
leave a legacy.

Chapter Four

WHY AREN'T WE READING THE BIBLE?

Houston, we have a problem.

If a believer is expected to read the Bible and meditate on what it says; if we are called to teach others what it says; then why do so many Christians have difficulty reading the Word of God? There seems to be a clear disconnect between what we say about the Bible and what we do.

Over many years, I have asked hundreds of people who regularly attend church to tell me about their own practice of reading the Bible. At first I was shocked by how many do not read the Bible even a little bit every day. On top of that, I was equally surprised by the fact that few could claim they had read the whole Bible, every verse.

Don't take my word for this (or studies done by professional survey groups). Ask around your church. I have asked a number of pastors about the Bible reading habits in their churches. They admit there is a problem. They just don't know what to do about it. So, they do what they can to teach from the pulpit.

> *I grew up a Christian, christened as a baby, raised in the church. It wasn't until I turned 50 that I read the Bible, Genesis to Revelation.*

Is Reading the Bible That Important?

One might ask whether reading the Bible is all that necessary, as long as a person believes what it says. I am guessing you saw the faulty logic in that sentence, as soon as you read it. How can a person believe a book which he has never read? Paul felt it important enough to mention this in his first letter to Timothy, verse 4:13,

> *"Until I come, give attention to the public reading of Scripture, to exhortation and teaching."*

Consider these questions. How does one put on the "whole armor of God" if parts of the armor are missing? How do we fulfill the Great Commission to teach another to observe everything the Lord commanded if we haven't read what he said? Should we expect our children to read the Bible if they don't see us doing it?

People who aren't believers feel no guilt about not reading the Bible. Why should they? Yet, when I ask believers about their own Bible reading practices, the look I see on their faces reveals their concern. Having neither read the whole Bible, nor having a habit of daily reading, they obviously regret their failure to do so. These questions are not about making people feel guilty. They simply expose a deep problem in the church today. People recognize that something is missing in their spiritual lives. They feel bad about it, but they don't know what to do.

Finding Compassion

In my research for *Point to Reading, Hope for the Future Through the Love of Reading,* I came to understand the root cause of why so few develop a love of reading. For many reasons, reading has been taught as a loveless exercise focused on workbooks and boring readers. Instead of the goal being the love of reading and how to understand and enjoy a great story, the focus has been grammar, vocabulary lists, and tests. Because of this error, two out of three students, fourth grade and above are reading below proficiency (according to national testing in 2011.[5]) These children become adults who dislike reading. Can you imagine them wanting to read the Bible?

If two out of three eighth graders cannot read proficiently, how can they possibly read Paul's letters (let alone the rest of the Bible) which demand a high level of reading ability? This problem of low reading proficiency is not a new one. My studies show that two out of three <u>adults</u> do not like to read. Here's the reason why. Many had their love of reading ruined when they were children. We are a nation where few like to read, and this lack of interest in reading has been passed down from parents to children, generation after generation.

Helping others become good readers takes compassion and patience. Compassion means having sympathy for the challenges they face.

Compassion literally means "to suffer with"—meeting them where they are and going through the learning process with them.

If you love to read, you can probably thank one of your parents, or another caring adult. But, just as the legacy of literacy can be passed down from one generation to the next, so can illiteracy. If we are going to change the future for our children (and the church), we must care enough to do what it takes to solve this very real tragedy. To develop Bible literacy in our children (and all believers), we must recognize the problems that are preventing this from happening.

Recognizing the Problems

According to surveys of national reading habits, nearly half of adults did not read a single book last year. Many studies reveal that as many as seven out of ten Americans simply don't like to read. Though most Americans know how to read, a perfect storm of unpleasant reading experiences causes most to simply give up. For many it is as early as first or second grade.

Bible Reading Problem #1:
The Bible is too hard for many people to read.

If eighth graders cannot read proficiently, how can we expect them to read a book as difficult as the Bible? With the strange names and customs from ancient cultures, it's understandable why most people don't try. It's easier to let the preacher or Sunday school teacher tell us what it says.

Bible Reading Problem #2:
Many people do not enjoy reading.

I've spoken with many about the love of reading. Teachers, parents, and children. Those who love to read were able to tell me why they love it. *"My mother (or father) read to me." "I grew up in a house full of books and everybody read." "I learned to read before I went to school."* They all had positive experiences with reading while were very young. And most were very good readers before they started school.

With two out of three adults in America not liking to read, that means many homes have no books. That means many children are not read to.

When they start school, they are not prepared to learn. Much of what they remember about school and reading is painful. They use words like: *boring, hard, tiring, a waste of time.* After years of *Hard & Boring*, are we surprised that they give up on reading and school by fourth grade?

Combine a low proficiency (an inability to read difficult books) with the reality that few enjoy reading, and it is easy to understand why so many can't find the time or desire to read anything, let alone the Bible.

These Two Problems Can Be Overcome...and easily

If people 1) haven't developed the ability to read the Bible, or 2) don't like to read, how can they possibly get past these problems to become a regular reader of the Word? By themselves, many never will. The answer can be found in one-on-one discipleship. Consider Philip's meeting with the Ethiopian described in Acts 8:30-31,

> *"Philip ran up and heard him reading Isaiah the prophet, and said, 'Do you understand what you are reading?' And he said, 'Well, how could I, unless someone guides me?' And he invited Philip to come up and sit with him."*

The answer to the problem of Bible reading is found in a mentor who can read, and has some understanding of the Bible. We need someone who will give of his time to help another understand and come to love reading the most important book ever written. Like Philip, you can be the guide who helps someone get past his or her resistance to reading.

But First!

It is important to recognize why anyone reads the Bible. Is it our own curiosity or intelligence which causes us to choose to know the Lord through His Word? In fact, the Bible tells us the exact opposite. In John 6:44, we read these words of Jesus:

> *"No one can come to Me, unless the Father who sent Me draws him; and I will raise him up on the last day."*

We understand that this desire to know the Lord and to read His Word happens because He first gives us the desire. Once the desire has been placed in our hearts, we must strive to overcome anything that might stop us from wanting to spend time with Him. Every believer fights this battle daily. We want to do what is right, but the desires of the world and our sin nature pull us the other way. Being born again does not make us perfect—it makes us "perfectable". The Lord has given us His Word for this process of sanctification. To benefit from the Bible, we must read and apply it. Obviously there is a headwind pushing against us, to keep us from making progress on that path of maturing in the faith. For this reason we must help each other stay in the Word.

Two Approaches for Two Different Kinds of People

Though the *PTR* way of building the love of reading is essentially the same for any situation, we will look at two slightly different approaches to working with these two different kinds of people.

1) The beginning reader This is the child (or adult) who does not know how to read well. Without help, the beginner struggles and may never get over the hill of difficulty. The simple instructions explained in the next chapter show you a fun and easy way to read the Bible with him. With *PTR* you become the mentor who gets him "over the hump" and on the road to becoming a person who enjoys reading the Bible.

While developing the skills of word identification (meaning of the words) and comprehension (meaning of the story), your friend does far more than simply learn to read. Using the *Point to Reading the Bible* way, you mentor him into the habit of regular Bible reading and the joy of understanding God's Word. [1] As mentor, you step into obedience of the Great Commission as you disciple him; [2] he steps into obedience of the command to read/hear/meditate on the Word on a daily basis. Can you think of a richer kind of Christian fellowship?

The problem of the Bible being too hard to read and understand is easily overcome when the beginning reader has an experienced reader to walk the path with him. The frustration that challenges every new reader is gone, because of you.

2) Those who can read, but don't like to do it Our churches are full of people who love the Lord but do not read the Bible. In the first *Point to Reading* book we examined the reasons why an estimated seven out of ten adults do not like to read.

1. No one read to them as children. They were unprepared to learn.
2. They experienced humiliation in school, which ruined their desire to learn to read.
3. The process of learning how to read took too long. Boredom and other distractions caused them to lose interest and quit.

Every person has a unique story with its own set of problems. Add a bunch of bad experiences and, in our minds, we create negative associations with reading. Once a person decides he is not smart enough, that reading is too hard, or that it just isn't worth the time and effort, should we be surprised he gives up? The Bible is difficult enough to read for the person who is a good reader and likes to read. Remove the joy and make it hard and it's no wonder so many Christians don't read their Bible.

As the mentor, it is your reading ability, your joy of reading, and your understanding of what the Bible stories mean that will carry your friend through the rough stages. Just like jumpstarting a car with a dead battery, it will be your love of reading the Bible that will jumpstart your friend's love of reading. As his own ability and understanding come alive, eventually he may choose to continue on his own.

> *The joy of reading is like a virus.*
> *Once infected, there is no known cure.*

The goal is for your friend to become one of those people who enjoy reading the Bible every day, growing in their faith and knowledge of who the Lord is and what He has done for us. Someday your disciple will be confident enough to share the blessing of the Word with another. You will know you have accomplished your mission (the Great Co-Mission) when he finds someone else and copies what you have done with him.

---

[5] http://nces.ed.gov/nationsreportcard/pubs/main2011/2012457.asp

Chapter Five

POINT TO READING INSTRUCTIONS

The point is to enjoy reading and learning.

We have looked at the effectiveness of Scripture *for teaching, for reproof, for correction, and for training in righteousness*. We discussed the value of building relationships through Bible reading, with the Lord and with others. We even considered how we can fulfill obedience to the Great Commission while leading others into obedience to read the Word. But, until we actually do it, all of this is talk with no results. No fruit. This chapter is about *ACTION*—becoming Doers of the Word.

Why do we want to read the Bible with our children and friends? **So they grow in understanding**. What will make them build a Bible-reading practice? **That they enjoy doing it**. Remove understanding and enjoyment and there's no point to reading. When I describe Point to Reading to someone for the first time, the common response is, "*That makes so much sense*." Let's start doing what makes sense, and stop with the *Hard & Boring*.

To achieve the goal of understanding and enjoyment, *PTR* works from a foundation of basic principles. These principles guiding the practice of *Point to Reading* are the same for the **beginning reader who does not read well**, as for the **person who can read, but doesn't**. In either case, you will be reading the Bible **with**, **not to**, the other person. Let's look at how these principles align with Scripture.

The Principles of *Point to Reading*™

1. Relationship
2. Fun & Easy
3. Setting a High Goal
4. Discussing the Story—*What does it mean?*
5. Encouragement—*"You can do this."*
6. Commitment—*Never giving up*

1. Relationship—*It's all about relationship!*

Who has not heard a pastor at some time say the Christian faith is not about rules, but relationship.

> *"By this all men will know that you are My disciples,*
> *if you have love for one another."* John 13: 35

This principle is placed at the top of the list. Everything we do with PTR is viewed through the lens of relationship. A simple question to ask:

> *Is what I'm doing helping or hindering relationship?*

If it improves relationship, do it. If it weakens relationship, don't. It is that simple. People have asked me all kinds of questions over the years. When I reply with this one question about relationship, the light comes on and they can see the right answer.

What kind of relationship do we mean? The one between you and the person you are mentoring, of course. Yet, this concept of relationship goes much deeper. We are creating a relationship with reading itself. Aren't we also building a relationship between your disciple and the Bible? And through the Bible aren't we fostering a relationship with the Lord? Is there anything that isn't about relationship?

2. Fun & Easy

Is our relationship with the Lord going to be very fruitful if it is not joyful? Consider what Jesus said in Matthew 11:30, *"For My yoke is easy, and My load is light."* And in the parable of the talents, the master told his faithful servant, *"Enter into the joy of your master."*

3. Setting a high goal

Goals are your meaningful purpose. A goal tells us where to aim, and when we have completed the task. The goal is your friend becoming a person who enjoys reading the Bible, understanding and obeying what it says. When will you know you've reached the goal? When daily Bible reading becomes his practice, and he starts discipling another.

> *"I press on toward the goal for the prize of the upward call*
> *of God in Christ Jesus."* Philippians 3:14

4. Discussing the story

Discussion is what helps the stories in the Bible make sense to the beginner. Your enthusiasm builds his interest. Your questions get him thinking about the meaning. Throughout the process, the Spirit of God is present to bring wisdom and understanding to each of you. The more he understands, the more he will want to learn. Discussion is true learning.

> *"You, however, continue in the things you have learned and become convinced of, knowing from whom you have learned them; and that from childhood you have known the sacred writings which are able to give you the wisdom that leads to salvation through faith which is in Christ Jesus. All Scripture is inspired by God and profitable for teaching, for reproof, for correction, for training in righteousness; that the man of God may be adequate, equipped for every good work."* 2 Tim 3:14-17

5. Encouragement

There could be a whole chapter just on the importance of encouraging each other, let alone the volume of verses which cover this principle.

> *"and let us consider how to stimulate one another to love and good deeds, not forsaking our own assembling together, as is the habit of some, but encouraging one another; and all the more, as you see the day drawing near."* Hebrews 10:24-25

6. Commitment

Commitment is the difference between those who start and those who finish. For the sake of those who are entrusted to your care, you be a person who finishes what he starts.

> *"Do you not know that those who run in a race all run, but only one receives the prize? Run in such a way that you may win."* 1 Corinthians 9:24

You may be wondering why I am spending so much time on this principle stuff. When I examine other *"This is the way we've always done* it" reading methods, I am amazed how they ignore these common sense principles as if they don't matter. Think for a moment about these six principles. Is there even one you would remove? Keep that in mind, because we will discuss the **PTR** way of Bible-reading discipleship in the light of all six principles.

Consider other ways the Bible is taught. Do those ways include these principles? When sitting in a classroom, listening to a lecture, does it feel relational? In other words, is it helping you build a relationship? Is it fun & easy, or hard & boring? In large groups, it can be uncomfortable or difficult to ask a lot of questions—so understanding suffers. Discussion is one of the keys to learning, but is so often overlooked. In a discipleship, it is encouragement and commitment that keeps the student coming back. **PTR the Bible** fulfills the goal of discipleship through Bible-reading, while not violating these principles. *And that is why it works so well.*

Two Different Approaches

Point to Reading the Bible was originally written and translated into Spanish as a tool for building literacy in Central and South America. Next it was published in English, the idea being to grow Bible knowledge as we teach our children to read. The lack of discipleship and general Bible knowledge in adult believers woke me up to the need for this book. It is now two books in one—for building both literacy and discipleship.

As mentioned earlier, there are two different approaches for two very different people you can mentor.

- The beginner (usually a child) who does not read well.
- Those who can read, but don't like to do it.

Little kids love books and want to learn how to read. Something along the way ruins their love of books and they turn into adults who have no interest in reading. Though the approach may look different for a young child compared to a mature adult, the principles work the same for both. We build a relationship with another while building our relationship with the Lord. Sounds a lot like *"love the Lord"* and *"love others as yourself"*. In either case, all you are doing is reading and discussing a good story.

When I explain the *PTR* concept, many think it is too simple to do any good. We think big problems need complex solutions. As you read these instructions, keep this in mind—all you'll be doing is reading the Bible with a friend and talking about what it says. Simple, yet very effective. Let's start with the person who knows how to read but doesn't read the Bible on his own.

Instructions for reading with someone who <u>can</u> read, but doesn't read the Bible

This may be your spouse or one of your children; a close friend or someone you hardly know. Don't be surprised how few read the Bible. Be aware that many people are sensitive about how well they read. Painful memories from being humiliated in elementary school are far more common than you may imagine. Many people avoid reading out loud because it is like public speaking, which most people avoid.

There may be many reasons your friend doesn't read the Bible. Most adults are not aware of why they don't like to read. Negative experiences from childhood get forgotten. They just know they don't like reading. Combine childhood embarrassment, the difficulty of understanding Biblical text, plus our own rebellious nature that fights against anything of God; is it surprising why people don't have the time or desire to read the Bible? Do not be deterred by their resistance. It will take time and your friendship to overcome these obstacles.

Be Patient

It is understandable why patience is one of the gifts of the Spirit. You will need to be patient with your disciple in Bible-reading. People tend to dislike things they don't do well. Your friend may feel that starting a habit of Bible-reading is like changing his diet or starting an exercise program. Your encouragement and example is needed to get him started until the habit becomes his own.

> *The spirit may be willing, but the flesh is certainly weak.*

The principles are the same as with the beginning reader

Relationship, Fun & Easy, Setting a High Goal, Discussing the Story, Encouragement and Commitment. We talk in church about fellowship. Here is an opportunity to build a fellowship based on Christ and the Bible. By stepping into obedience to the Great Commission, we support another into obedience through reading and meditating on His Word.

A relationship without fun or a meaningful purpose is one that will not go far. A quality relationship demands encouragement and commitment. All these principles are essential to a healthy and enjoyable friendship.

Getting started

Since your friend already knows how to read, it may be helpful for each of you to have your own Bible. Pointing his finger to the word he is reading improves focus and attention.

> ➢ Read a verse, then talk about what it means. Take turns being the reader, so that he is not always the "reader" or just the "listener".
> ➢ Ask questions. When you first start reading together, he may not have answers. After reading together for a while, the thoughts will come. He may even start asking questions. In time, sharing his ideas with you will become easier. Be patient.
> ➢ "Discussing the story" is an opportunity to share something you heard in a sermon on the particular verse or story you are reading. You can also say how this verse has impacted your life.

REMEMBER: Lecturing is not the same as having a discussion.

A Bible dictionary helps with comprehension. You can explain the meaning, as you understand it. And it's okay to say "I don't know". Do research to find the answer for the next time you come together. Your friend will appreciate your effort, plus you demonstrate a good habit of looking things up. Always remember to ask the *Source of All Wisdom*. The Bible tells us to pray and ask God for answers. He desires for us to know the truth. Ask Him.

Never skip a word or idea your friend doesn't understand.

Choosing where to begin

Ask your friend if he has a book of the Bible that interests him. Depending on how much time you want to spend reading together, you could read part of a story and then finish with a Psalm or a section of Proverbs. One fun thing is to read the "Proverbs for the day". There are thirty-one chapters in Proverbs—one for every day of the month. There is no "wrong way" to begin reading the Bible, as long as you do it.

Be sensitive to the workings of the Spirit

The wonderful thing about relationships is what can happen as we build trust with each other. A particular passage of Scripture may bring up a memory in your friend's life that he wants to talk about. There may be something going on in his life at that moment which he wants to discuss with you. The sharing of important issues is the privilege of trusted friendship. This is one way that Christian fellowship becomes meaningful. It does not mean you become a counselor. Jesus is our Counselor. Just being a friend who listens is a powerful testimony. Let the Word of God be the guide and teacher.

How often should you get together?

As often as you can and he is willing. If this is your child in your home, you can set aside a few minutes any morning or night. Remember, you want to encourage a Bible-reading habit. Do as much as you can to build the positive habit, but not so much that your child feels like it is too much and he resents the time. This is where the principles of relationship help us make the right decision. Be sensitive to the other person.

Who should I ask to read the Bible with me?

It can be a person at work on your lunch break. Or a friend you meet after work. This is a fine way to start a friendship with a neighbor, or deepen a relationship with someone at church. Use the break between services on Sunday morning. You may be amazed how much Bible you can read, and the quality of relationship you might build by committing to spending that time with someone every Sunday over a period of time. But before going to an acquaintance, consider your spouse and children. They are our primary responsibility. Start at home.

"*How do I invite someone to read the Bible with me?*"

For some people the most difficult part of starting a Bible-reading discipleship will be getting started. I hope you won't let the nervousness of asking be what stops you from doing this. A simple question works.

- *"Have you ever done a Bible-reading fellowship?"*
- *"I have been wanting to find someone to read the Bible with me. Is that something you would enjoy?"*
- *"Would you like to use the break between services to read the Bible with me? Or maybe over lunch after church?"*

The worst that can happen is they say, "NO!" And they also may say "YES". I hope you will take the risk and get it started.

You can do this.

> **Without relationship and meaning, words would be no more than black marks on a piece of paper.**

Reading is about relationship. A relationship you build while reading the Bible with your friend—studying relationships described in the Bible stories—and each of you building your own relationship with the Lord. Through all of this time together, your relationship with the Lord will be the spark which helps to light the fire in your friend.

NEXT STEPS

In time, when your friend has reached a level of strong reading ability and understanding, you might introduce him to a group which meets regularly. He will be welcomed and acknowledged for his growth.

This is not the time to discontinue your Bible time together. Never lose sight of the importance of the relationship the two of you have built in the time you have shared learning and loving God's Word together. Continue to encourage him in his faith and knowledge of the Lord.

Start your own group

At this point you have already started a group—the two of you. Some day you might like to invite someone you know to join you. This can be a good idea, but I would wait until your friend is already strong in his habit and practice of Bible-reading. It may be that the nature of your relationship means the two of you want to stay just the two of you.

Starting at home first

In Acts 1:8, the disciples were told, "*you will be my witnesses in Jerusalem and in all Judea and Samaria, and to the end of the earth.*" Was he not telling them (and us) to take care of the home before going out into the community, and before witnessing to the rest of the world? Are we husbands not given instruction to "*wash our wives with the water of the Word*"? It was on purpose that the very first verse quoted in this book is Deuteronomy 6:7, commanding us to teach our children.

Why are these instructions to mentor our wives and children so important? Besides the obvious—*God said so*—there is the reason of legacy. What you do with your children...they will do with your grandchildren. And if they follow your example, the training of your descendants in the love and respect for the Lord may never end. If you miss this opportunity, the warning of Judges 2 (that Israel forgot the Lord and all He had done for them) may come to your family. Could this be what has happened in America?

The concept of legacy also applies to reading the Bible with our spouses. If you have children, what you do with your spouse is a witness to them by your example. Our children copy us. If we want them to build their future marriages on the foundation of the Word, we must lead by example. There is no more effective way to teach our children than by what we do. And yet it amazes me that parents would think their children will do anything but copy what they see their parents do.

Your children are watching.
They want to become just like you.

Instructions for the Beginning Reader

Forgive me for how often I repeat this—*It's all about relationship.* Many grew up with reading experiences that were humiliating and boring. Do we want to copy those mistakes with another? Old habits die hard, which is why the constant reminders. Make reading a fun time and a beginner can enjoy reading anything, even the Bible. Make it hard or unpleasant and beginners want to quit. Following the common sense principles of relationship, you make it fun and easy.

The way of reading and discussing the story is the same for beginners as for those who already can read. The only difference is getting your beginner through the initial stage of learning how to read.

Give your friend a Bible if he doesn't have one. Use a regular adult Bible to build a strong reading ability.

Find your reading spot. Sit in a comfortable, quiet, well-lit room. Avoid potential distractions. For people outside of your family, you can do this at church, or in a room with others.

If possible, bring a Bible dictionary (or computer). The practice of looking up words will make a difference in understanding and enjoying the stories.

Point and Say. Holding the Bible in front of both of you, point with your finger to the first word. If he knows the word, he says it. If he doesn't know the word, you immediately say it and move your finger to the next word. Let the sentences flow so that they make sense. (*More will be said about this later.*)

Discuss the Story, verse by verse. Discussion builds understanding. This is important. Do not hurry, but instead focus on the message. Discussion is the core of *PTR*, and the foundation for real learning. Getting your person to talk brings him into active participation, and it grows your relationship.

> ➢ With you as his guide, instead of struggling and feeling embarrassed, he gets to enjoy the story with you. Reading together, your friend finds out how easy reading can be.

> ➢ With your discussions of what the stories mean, your friend discovers the wisdom and beauty of God's Word. Instead of confusion because he doesn't understand, he learns.

PTR is different from what we used to do.

1. Make it Fun & Easy (No Torture)

☑ **No reading out loud in front of large groups of people**. Public speaking is scary. *PTR* is done one-on-one; you and your friend without an audience.

☑ **No sounding out words during *PTR***. Having to sound out words is torture to a beginning reader. Plus, it interrupts the story. How can a beginner understand the sentence while figuring out how to say a word? The Bible has plenty of words and names that can be a distraction. Let him say the words he knows; you say all the rest. In time, he will learn all the words. The main thing is to prevent embarrassment. Now is the time for enjoyment.

2. It's About the Story!

☑ **Let the sentence flow**. You are reading a story, not practicing word pronunciation. A story is understood in sentences, not separate words.

☑ **Read the whole sentence, word by word**. At first, he may only read one or two words out of each sentence. You read all the other words; be sure to keep the sentence flowing. I REPEAT: this isn't about learning to read; it's about understanding a story.

47

> *The story adds to the meaning of the words just like the words add to the meaning of the story.*

☑ **Never skip a word or idea your friend doesn't understand**. Very important. Skipping words we do not understand ruins comprehension. Use a dictionary, if necessary.

☑ **Focus on the meaning of the story**. Make sure he understands each sentence. Read a sentence again if it helps him understand. Don't hurry, but keep it going so the sentences and story make sense.

☑ **Ask questions: "What do you think this means?" "What is God wanting us to learn?"** Discussing the meaning of the story builds comprehension and enjoyment. You may find yourself reading only a chapter during a session. That is okay. One verse can change a person's life. What matters is understanding the story. This makes reading a joy, for both of you.

Remember: the point is __not__ how fast we can read the Bible. It's how much we understand and enjoy.

3. Take Turns Being the Active Reader

Have your beginner "read" (with your help) one section, saying only the words he knows. Then let him listen and watch while you read another section, ***still pointing to each word.*** Then have him read another section with you. This is the pattern you will use as he gradually grows his ability. As his ability and vocabulary increase, let him read longer sections, until he is reading half and then a whole passage. Continue to give him a break so he can just listen and enjoy the story. What matters most is his joy in the time with you in the Word. Keep discussing what you are learning in the story. Never sacrifice understanding for speed, as if you have to finish so many verses or chapters in a day.

48

Why do we switch back and forth?

There's a big difference between active reading and passive listening. For a person who has never learned how to read, being able to take turns removes the pressure of having to do all the work. Instead of the shock of suddenly being expected to do 100% active reading, the *PTR* way allows your friend to gradually ease into active reading. He becomes an active reader at his own pace.

> ➤ The pressure of performance is removed.
> ➤ Since active reading is "work", he won't experience "burn-out" from having to do all the reading.
> ➤ When you read, he can relax and just focus on enjoying the story, though his mind will continue to learn words as he looks where your finger is pointing and listens to your voice.
> ➤ He gets a demonstration of how correct reading sounds.
> ➤ The enjoyment of the shared experience builds confidence.

<u>Remember:</u> It's about discovering the Bible's wisdom and hearing the Lord's voice, not "learning to read".

4. Point and Say

When it is your friend's turn to be the active reader, you point to each word and he says all the words he knows. PLEASE: Do not make him sound out the word he doesn't know. This distracts from having his focus on the story. A person can't be sounding out a word and thinking about its meaning at the same time. You immediately say it and move on. Make sure to discuss unknown words.

The topic of sounding out words has been controversial. Sounding out words is a valuable skill, just like learning to cook is useful for eating. At some point, we must stop "cooking" and enjoy the meal. If we are going to build a love for reading the Bible, we must set aside the tedious exercises and allow a person to enjoy the story.

Be patient with your beginner.

It's a slow process when you start. It may sound funny as you read most of the words in a sentence with him popping in with only "the" and "a". To a beginner, reading anything is a huge accomplishment. As the weeks and months go by, your friend will steadily add new words. One day, he'll be reading every word on the page and you'll both be amazed at how quickly it happened.

5. Use Positive Reinforcement

Regularly encourage your friend by saying: *"You can do this."* As he reads new words, say things like: *"Good job." "Excellent." "You are good at this."*

This is not false praise. You are telling the truth. Each time he reads a word, <u>*he is doing well*</u>. This is reinforcing the fact that he can (and will) be a good reader. Celebrate each success. He will learn that reading is fun and easy. By the time he finishes the Bible, he will have a belief in his reading based on the truth—that he is a very good reader.

> <u>*Remember*</u>: *You don't need to say something after every word he reads. A few times in a section is enough. Do it when he reads a word for the first time, or reads a word he has not seen in a while. Encouragement makes him want to keep trying.*

6. It's About the Relationship—Reading is Relational

Your relationship with your friend is important to the learning process. Some people think the Bible is just about rules. Others understand how our faith is about relationship—with the Lord and with each other. The Bible tells stories of people like Abraham, Joseph, Moses and David who had very close relationships with the Lord. The relationship you enjoy with your friend while the two of you read the Bible together is a reflection of the relationship he can have with the Lord while reading His Word. Also, remember Jesus sent out his disciples by two's. One may have been a more experienced disciple, yet together they could encourage each other as they faced challenges in their work.

7. Commitment

Be consistent. Stay with it by making sure you read regularly. The regular and frequent reading times allow your beginner to learn very quickly. This is also very important for understanding the meaning of the stories. You don't have to read every day; but do as much as you can. You want to encourage and build the habit of daily Bible reading.

Finish what you have started

Remember the Goal: your friend loving and understanding the Word.
- ☑ Able to read and understand what the Bible says
- ☑ Wanting to read the Bible on his own
- ☑ Someday committing to reading with another person

You will know when your friend is succeeding because he will read well. Once he is confident in his ability, encourage him to read at home on his own. Maybe in the morning when he wakes, or before he goes to sleep at night. You can also encourage him to read with his family or a friend. That will bless the others while building confidence in his reading ability. Remember, the ultimate goal is not just reading on his own. When he steps into the role of mentoring another, he expands the kingdom by fulfilling the Great Commission.

In case you think it might be beyond the ability of a beginning reader to share the love of reading with another, I offer this story. Years back, I taught *Point to Reading* to teachers and parents at a Christian K-12 school. As a way of teaching by example, I offered to read with a new student. Though already in second grade, he was doing poorly in reading. When I first met him, I asked what his favorite subject is. His face brightened up as he said, "Science". Next session I brought a high school level book with amazing photos covering a broad range of general science topics. Though challenging, he loved the material and enjoyed the attention. In just a few months, this *"boy who couldn't read"* was improving dramatically.

One day his teacher pulled me aside, "Mr. Larsen, guess what I caught our boy doing? I found him sitting with a kindergartner, reading with her the *Point to Reading* way." All by himself, he shared his love of reading with another by simply doing what I had done with him.

THE START, MIDDLE AND END OF *PTR* READING TIME

Starting to read the Bible For the beginner who knows few words, it will be enough for him to follow the story and say the words he knows as you point to them. Discuss the meaning as you go verse by verse. As time passes, his vocabulary will increase. Hearing a word he already knows (which your finger is pointing to), he will connect the look of the word with its sound. Focus on the meaning of the story and his understanding—his brain will do the job of figuring out the words. Encourage often; congratulate regularly.

> *With PTR, a beginner reads at his own level while you help him understand the story. In time his ability catches up with what you are reading. Be patient.*

Consider starting with the Gospels to learn about Jesus and his message. Then the Old Testament will be easier to understand. Genesis, Exodus and the book of Judges are good because they are full of stories about people. Proverbs and Psalms offer opportunity for good discussion. Focus on the people and what we can learn from their lives. Best of all, choose any story you are passionate about. It is your passion that will catch his attention. Our joy can be contagious.

In the Middle As the months go by, the words he knows will increase to the point that he'll read whole verses by himself. If he does not understand commas and periods, now is a good time to tell him, "*You pause at a comma and take a breath at a period.*" With practice, he'll get the hang of it. Listening to you read, he will learn how it should sound.

Much of the Bible is like poetry. Reading with you will help him appreciate the beauty of Scripture. Help him learn to sing the sentences. Kids can talk just fine. But when they read, it is often with the same flat tone, one word after another. Listening to you read teaches him how to make the sentences sing. He'll learn to go up with his voice at the end of a question, and down when it's the end of a statement. There's no point trying to teach rules here—he already knows how conversation sounds.

Simply show how the sentence is supposed to sound. Every once in a while, have him read a sentence again so he can hear himself getting it right. Remember to encourage and congratulate. *"You're doing great!"*

At the End of Each Session Finish up your reading time with a short discussion about the story. What did he learn? What is God telling him with this story? Get him talking about what the story means to him. You can even share what the story means to you.

> *"But what does it say? 'The word is near you, in your mouth and in your heart'—that is, the word of faith which we are preaching, that if you confess with your mouth Jesus as Lord, and believe in your heart that God raised Him from the dead, you shall be saved; for with the heart man believes, resulting in righteousness, and with the mouth he confesses, resulting in salvation."* Romans 10:8-10

> **This may be the most important part of what you will do while reading the Bible together. It is not what you teach him that will cause him to learn, but what the Holy Spirit puts in his heart which he speaks from his mouth. Discussion matters.**

At the Beginning of the Next Session Before you start reading, ask what was happening the last time you read together. This brief moment reconnects him to the story, builds comprehension and improves communication skills. After he finishes telling you what he remembers, get started with that day's reading.

A Recap

1. When you begin, remember what you learned the last session.
2. Read and discuss today's stories.
3. Talk about what you and your student have discovered from today's reading.

There Will Come a Day

Before Jesus left his earthly ministry, he gave his disciples a mission. The Lord had lived with the twelve for three years, teaching and preparing them for the day when they would go out and do what He had taught them to do. Matthew 28:18-20

> *"And Jesus came up and spoke to them, saying,*
> *'All authority has been given to Me in heaven and on earth.*
> *Go therefore and make disciples of all the nations, baptizing*
> *them in the name of the Father and the Son and the Holy*
> *Spirit, teaching them to observe all that I commanded you;*
> *and lo, I am with you always, even to the end of the age.'"*

Look to that day when your disciple will be ready to find someone to encourage. Then his learning can take the next step, as he obediently fulfills the Great Commission himself. And why will your disciple take this step? Because this is what you showed by your example.

> *We teach by example.*
> *We learn by copying what we are shown.*

Chapter Six

A MESSAGE TO CHURCH ELDERS

Leading the church into fulfilling all righteousness

We must not hold back from helping each other to grow Bible-reading and discipleship in the church. We know something is missing, and yet the problem is so big and seems impossible to solve. A common response seems to be to pretend this isn't a problem, or tell ourselves we are doing all that we can. But, are we?

Are Bible-reading and discipleship minor points of faith?

Are these basic to the faith and growth of every believer? How well can a person grow in his faith without a personal practice of Bible-reading? Is discipleship a command given to us by the Lord, or is it simply a suggestion that we can follow or not, as we choose? Could the absence of these two components be preventing believers from growing to maturity?

> *"For there is no good tree which produces bad fruit;*
> *nor, on the other hand, a bad tree which produces good fruit.*
> *For each tree is known by its own fruit."* Luke 6:43-44a

> *"By this is my Father glorified, that you bear much fruit,*
> *and so prove to be My disciples."* John 15:8

There are many ways that a follower of Jesus can bear fruit. These two Bible verses are not offered to suggest that Bible-reading causes salvation or makes believers. But, it does reveal a desire to build a relationship.

Bible-reading and discipleship are components of building a relationship with the Lord. Bible reading can be the way to disciple others, guiding them into their own relationship.

What are considered the greatest commandments? Love the Lord, and love others as yourself. Relationship.

Since the act of making disciples seems to be commanded, should we disregard the Great Commission as optional for any and all believers? Simply reading the Bible does not, in itself, change a person's life. We must do as James advises, to be doers of the word and not hearers only. Instead, might we consider Bible-reading and discipleship to be signs of maturity in the walk of a believer?

How do we help our children grow to maturity?

When they are infants, we do for them. Why? Because they do not know what to do for themselves. Part of our job as parents is to teach them, and then encourage them to take on responsibility and do for themselves. We put the food in their mouths. When they are ready, we show them how to hold the spoon and allow them to feed themselves (*cleaning up their messes after them*). We teach them how to put on their clothing, initially doing it with them. Over time we allow them to do more and more for themselves. Eventually we expect our children to work and pay for their own food and clothing. These are signs of their maturity—that they take on these duties when they are ready. We know we have done the job correctly when they do it on their own.

On the contrary, if our children refuse to do what is expected of them, what do we do? Some parents do what is needed to help their children to "grow up". Other parents make excuses for their kids, continuing to do for their adult children (*is that an oxymoron?*) those things they should be doing for themselves. This lack of correct action of both the parents and children weakens the family, besides the fact that the children do not mature and become responsible citizens.

> *"For though by this time you ought to be teachers, you have need again for someone to teach you the elementary principles of the oracles of God, and you have come to need milk and not solid food. For everyone who partakes only of milk is not accustomed to the word of righteousness, for he is an infant."* Hebrews 5:12-13

And what is this *"word of righteousness"*? Is it not the Bible? Can we become mature in the faith if we do not know what it says?

Leading our children into maturity

As leaders in the church—those who are mature in the faith—do we have a responsibility to teach and encourage our children in the faith? Every person and every church must decide whether the practices of Bible-reading and discipleship are necessary to the faith, or can be considered voluntary. For those who believe these are essential to the Christian walk, let us do what is needed to develop these practices in all church members.

Show, not just tell

Pastors may say, "*I regularly tell the church about the importance of Bible-reading.*" That is good, but children need more than to be told. They need to be shown. In the beginning, they need someone to come alongside them and help them do it. The nature of discipleship is doing something *WITH* people, helping them do it, until they are able to do it all by themselves. We hold children up in the pool as they learn how to swim. We ride *WITH* them while they are learning how to drive. We understand the importance of things that are a life & death matter like driving or swimming. Are not Bible-reading and discipleship also matters of life and death? Pastor, imagine the joy of preaching to people who read the Bible, know what it says, and obey its instructions.

The Hope of *Point to Reading the Bible*

I imagine a day when our churches are full of people who read their Bible because they love to read it and make it a part of their daily lives. I look to that day when discipleship is part of the fellowship between the old and young, and between the mature and new believer. I call on elders in the church to take a stand for these two pillars of our faith.

> *I imagine a day when our churches are full of people who read their Bible, and where discipleship is a regular part of the fellowship between the old and young, the mature and new.*

I have written this book to encourage every believer to step out in obedience to the Great Commission and find one person to mentor in the love of reading the Bible. Though most of the book is written to the individual, I hope to encourage churches to disciple their members in the way of Bible reading for disciple-fellowship. Here are some suggestions for how this can be accomplished.

1. The first step is for all believers to take seriously our own responsibility to disciple others.
2. Next, the leaders of our churches agree and commit to Bible reading for the process of maturing in the faith.
3. Finally, we commit time for it. If something is important, we will figure out how to make it happen.

When can we fit this Bible-reading fellowship into our already crowded church service schedules?

What church doesn't have a busy schedule? When can we make time for this? How about the break between services on Sunday morning? Or after the service is over? If everyone were to sit down in the sanctuary with one other person and read together for just fifteen minutes, consider the impact this would have in just a few years.

It's tempting to think, *"We are already doing that in our Bible-study sessions."* Yes, classes expand Bible knowledge, but do they show people how to disciple others? Do they build one-to-one relationships? As stated elsewhere, do we want our churches full of students or teachers?

This is not to suggest that what we are presently doing is wrong. But, are we fulfilling the commands we claim to believe we should obey? Could we be doing better? If older and mature believers were to partner with young and new members, we could step into obedience to the Great Commission—to the mature teaching the new believer, and a real demonstration of the brethren loving others as they do themselves. In time we would have a transformation of our churches, through deeper fellowships and greater maturity in our walk.

A necessary component is relationship. That means the same two people come together each week over many months. This is not just about learning to read or learning what the Bible says. It's about forming relationships in a deep and meaningful way. Through obedience to disciple as our Lord commands, the church in America will become an irresistible force in the world.

Revival

Every day, current events cry out about the need for revival, and specifically revival in the church. We are saddened when another nationally known church leader falls into sin. We despair over the fact that an overwhelming majority of our youth abandon the church when they leave home. Are we powerless to do anything about it?

> *"For it is time for judgment to begin with the household of God;*
> *And if it begins with us first, what will be the outcome for those*
> *who do not obey the Gospel of God?*
> *And if it is with difficulty that the righteous is saved,*
> *What will become of the godless man and the sinner?"*
> 1 Peter 4:17-18

Can there be nationwide revival without the Bible?

It is easy to complain about the moral decay in our country. It is easy to point the finger at the leader who has fallen. It is amazing to me that anyone should want to step out as a leader, considering how our leaders have become targets for attack on all levels. Where will our leaders come from if we do not train people in the truth of the Word? What hope is there for the church as a force for good in the world if we do not put on the full armor of God, which includes the Sword? One truth of warfare is that an army marches on its stomach. An army without food cannot fight.

> *But he answered and said, "It is written, 'Man shall not live*
> *on bread alone, but on every word that proceeds*
> *out of the mouth of God.'"* Matthew 4:4

Since Jesus turned to Scripture to battle the temptations of the Devil, would it not be wise for us to follow his example.

Chapter Seven

REVIVAL: A CALL TO ACTION

*Remember: There will come a day when
all that will matter of our efforts is
what we have taught our children.*

Many would like to read the Bible, but don't. We want to do what the Lord calls us to do, but find it hard to get started. Or we do things which don't seem to produce much fruit. This book, this idea called Point to Reading, is a simple yet effective way for the church and believers to accomplish many important aspects of our faith.

1. Fulfill **obedience** to the Great Commission effectively.
2. Build **fellowship** among believers that can grow into deeper relationships.
3. Increase Bible **knowledge** in both new and mature believers.
4. Break down walls between age groups, **sharing the wisdom** of older and mature Christians.
5. Fulfill the command of Deuteronomy 6 to **teach our children**.
6. Create a **legacy of doing**, where our children learn to be obedient because they see us being obedient.
7. Start a **revival** in the church, which will impact the world.

We have plenty of excuses for seeing no action in these points.

- Too busy;
- Don't know the Bible well enough;
- Don't know how to teach;
- *"It's the pastor's job"*.

When we let our excuses control us, it's easy to get stuck in a rut of doing only what is comfortable for us. But, if that old way is not getting us any better results (aka fruit), then we ought to consider doing something different. Doing something different is the key to getting different results.

Let's review these seven impacts that we can have on ourselves and others by following this call for reading the Bible together. Isn't it amazing how the simple act of reading and discussing the Bible with someone can have a life-changing impact on everyone involved?

1. Obedience to the Great Commission
2. Building Fellowship
3. Increasing Bible Knowledge
4. Sharing Wisdom between the generations
5. Teaching our children
6. Create a Legacy of Doing
7. Start a Revival in the Church

And He said to him, " 'You shall love the Lord your God with all your heart, and with all your soul, and with all your mind.' This is the great and foremost commandment. The second is like it, 'You shall love your neighbor as yourself.' On these two commandments depend the whole Law and the Prophets."
Matthew 22:37-40

Should we consider these seven to be commands? Some might agree. If not commands, could they be more than good suggestions? Are there any you would want left out of your church's mission statement?

We are in the middle of a spiritual war.

There are countries which have been at war for so long that its citizens, and especially their children, have grown up knowing nothing but war. Peace is an intellectual concept that only exists in other places. We are a people who live in a world of continual war.

We were born into a world of spiritual warfare that has been going on for thousands of years. It is easy to forget the reality of warfare when we get wrapped up in the day-to-day business of work and survival. And yet we have been called to something much higher than worrying about what we will eat and what we will wear. The reality of this spiritual war is that we are surrounded by the lies and temptations of the enemy. It is this enemy's hope that we will forget the commandments of the Lord.

Satan hopes we do 1) *not fulfill* the Great Commission, 2) *not build* Christian fellowship, 3) *not increase* Bible knowledge, 4) *not break down the age barriers*, opening our youth to learning from older, wiser adults, 5) *not teach* our children, 6) so that our enemy can *prevent a legacy of action* where our children learn from our obedience, and 7) therefore accomplish his goal of *preventing true revival* in the world.

"He who is not with Me is against Me; and
he who does not gather with Me scatters." Matthew 12:30

None of this is to suggest that a discipleship of reading the Bible with another is the only way to be a follower of Christ. Nor will this be without effort. Many things in life are simple, yet worthy goals take some work. The enemy's methods of spiritual warfare are designed to prevent us from doing the very things we know we should, wish we could, but don't.

"For what I am doing, I do not understand;
for I am not practicing what I would like to do,
but I am doing the very thing I hate." Romans 7:15

Life is often like a storm. Obeying the commands of the Lord can be like trying to walk against a strong wind. The demands of the world will fill up every waking moment...if we allow it. It is only through the power of God's spirit and concerted effort on our part that we will go in the right direction. God is willing. It is therefore up to us to set aside the time, if we want to see revival in our churches and in our lives.

This world can be a difficult and unpleasant place. Can we change the world? I think not, as thousands of years of history will testify. But, we can make a difference in the life of one person.

"I am only one, but still I am one. I cannot do everything,
but I can do something; and because I cannot do everything,
I will not refuse to do something I can do." *Helen Keller*

What will you do with this book?

What will you do with your time?

If you agree with the ideas in this book, will you help another grow in his spiritual walk? If you believe this is a worthy use of your time, here are some suggestions of what you can do now.

1. Think of someone you would like to get to know better, and invite him or her to read the Bible with you.
2. Take this book to your pastor and church leaders. Ask them to read it. Then ask if this would be a good step for your church.
3. Give the book to a friend. Let's get a movement of Bible reading discipleship going in our country.
4. Start first at home. Read and discuss with your spouse. Do the same with your children while they still live at home with you.

> *My wife and I regularly make time to read a few chapters of the Bible. Sometimes in the morning or at night before sleep. We are amazed by how much we continue to learn.*

A Bible-based Revival

If this country is going to see life-changing revival, will it start with dynamic pastors and popular teachers? Will it come from the growth of mega churches which offer a multitude of services—from youth centers to coffee bars? Will revival be due to Christian youth camps or concerts with awesome music and light shows? Will social (most of which is anti-social) media or blockbuster movies make it happen?

> ### *If revival were to come from what we are already doing, would it not already be here?*

Though social media is new on the scene (this generation), all the other ways of spreading the gospel have existed for fifty years or more. If you attempt to unlock a door, believing you already have the key, how many times will you repeatedly try the same key before realizing the key you need is not on that keychain?

Your own church may be growing in many wonderful ways, but the country, in general, is not. The Pew Research Center's 2014 Religious Landscape Study tells us "there are strong signs that many are less certain about this belief [in God] than in years past. And a small but growing minority of Americans say they do not believe in God at all."[6]

> *"The changes have been even more substantial when it comes to certainty of belief in God: 63% of Americans are absolutely certain that God exists, **down 8 percentage points from 2007**, when 71% said this."*[7]

Since one focus of this book is discipling the young, the following quote from the Pew Research Center is especially troubling.

> *"But perhaps the most striking divide – and the driving force behind the overall drop in belief – is generational. As younger Americans enter adulthood, they are far less likely to be sure about God's existence than are their elders. While 70% of those ages 65 and older express an absolutely certain belief in God or a universal spirit, only about half of adults under 30 feel the same way (51%)."*[8]

Even with a heavy emphasis in the church on youth evangelism, the facts tell us that what we are doing is not working. The Pew Research study gives us a second witness on this matter.

> *"Pew Research Center surveys are not the only ones that have found a long-term decline in the overall share of Americans who say they believe in God. For example, 86% of Americans said <u>in a 2014 Gallup poll</u>[9] they believed in God or a universal spirit, down from 96% in 1994 and the lowest figure since Gallup first asked the question in 1976."*

Remember in Judges when Israel turned to other gods because the message wasn't taught to the next generation? We are that generation. But we aren't without hope. King Josiah read the Word of God to his people at a low point in Judea's history, bringing revival. Will we also turn and do what is right in God's eyes?

Fulfilling the Great Commission

We understand the Great Commission commands us to make disciples. If we are going to be obedient to teach others to *"observe all that I* [the Lord] *commanded you"*, is it enough to tell them what He said? The answer is in the word *observe*. Observe can mean to look at something. But in Matthew 28, we are commanded into action. This *observe* means we are to *know and do*. First we must **know** all that He has commanded. Then we are to **do** them. Do we fulfill this command by inviting people to church so someone else can disciple them? Are evangelism and discipleship the same thing? I do not believe so. When Jesus taught his disciples, we know he intended for each of them to go and make disciples. Jesus told his disciples, *"If you love me, keep my commandments."* Isn't this a command to obey the Great Commission, itself?

Here is the exciting part. When will anyone know he has fulfilled the Great Commission? Won't the work be finished when his student goes out and starts discipling another? We know we are to be *"doers of the word, and not merely hearers only"*. Following our Lord also means following his example. We are to complete the job of discipleship, which means staying with it until our friend steps out in faith to teach another.

Won't This Take a Long Time?

Discipleship may seem like an inefficient use of a teacher's time. One person teaching twenty is a good plan for offering information. But, it is not discipleship. Our Lord commanded us to use his method to grow people in the faith, and make disciples who would make even more disciples. Why did Jesus choose this method?

Making disciples is work, but it is important, even necessary, work.
1. We are teaching by example.
2. Working with one person, a teacher can be sure the message is understood. This can easily be missed in a large group.
3. The personal attention builds the relationship. We are modeling the one-to-one relationship our Lord has with us.

Our commitment to the relationship, plus our obedience to the Great Commission, helps our friend/disciple stay with the work until it's done.

Should we be "doing discipleship" any other way than the Lord's way?

The importance of a mentor/coach   I have a "smart phone" which often makes me feel stupid. Starting to use my phone was hard because it was new and foreign to me. But when a friend showed me how, I was able to start using it. Many things seem much harder in the beginning than they really are. A helper makes the learning process a lot easier.

The power of relationship   Your presence may be the difference in whether your friend succeeds or fails. Many people prefer eating a meal or watching a movie with a friend. You demonstrate your relationship with the Lord in the relationship you offer your friend.

Your joy is contagious.   Regardless of what we say, people learn from our example. Your love of reading the Bible will be one of the important messages your friend receives from this time together.

It starts slow, but in time it bears much fruit.

Is our ultimate goal in teaching another to make him into a student or a teacher? Discipleship is about making student-teachers. It is our own example of study which encourages another to become a lifelong student of the Bible. It is also our example which encourages them to disciple another. Though it may take many months with one person, in time that student can disciple another. One becomes two; two become four. In a few short years, through discipleship, a teacher may facilitate dozens of teachers instead of a room full of students.

This does not mean discipleship is to replace teaching to groups. Jesus spoke to the 5,000, but he put much of his time into his disciples. By following His example, with patience, we will bear much fruit. May you be greatly blessed as you obediently share your love of the Bible.

A Final Thought on Matthew 28:20

I have spent years pondering these few verses known as the Great Commission. Up until recently, I did not recognize how the last part fit in with the rest of the passage. How does this verse meaningfully connect to what came before it?

"and lo, I am with you always, even to the end of the age."

Then one day, it struck me that Jesus was telling us the rest of the story. Could it be he is saying that as we fulfill this commandment, he will be right there with us? And then I was reminded of his words:

"For where two or three have gathered together in My name, there I am in their midst." Matt 18:20

Now, go and make disciples.

"On that day the deaf will hear words of a book, and out of their gloom and darkness the eyes of the blind will see. The afflicted also will increase their gladness in the Lord, and the needy of mankind will rejoice in the Holy One of Israel." Isaiah 29:18-19

---

6   http://www.pewresearch.org/fact-tank/2015/11/04/americans-faith-in-god-may-be-eroding/
7   http://www.pewresearch.org/fact-tank/2015/11/04/americans-faith-in-god-may-be-eroding/
8   http://www.pewresearch.org/fact-tank/2015/11/04/americans-faith-in-god-may-be-eroding/
9 http://www.gallup.com/poll/1690/Religion.aspx

Resources and Study Guides

These are examples of books I use for reference. Through the internet you can find many others. And there is an app for just about anything.

Who Was Who in the Bible © 1999 Thomas Nelson Publishers

The Strongest Strong's Exhaustive Concordance of the Bible
James Strong, LL.D., S.T.D. Copyright © 2001 by Zondervan

I thank the pastors and teachers who have been a source of inspiration and knowledge. Dozens on the radio challenged me to grow in the faith. God bless Pastors Charles, Gary, and Jim for their efforts to lead their churches, and who contributed to my understanding. With gratitude I acknowledge Susan who patiently put up with me in my office under the excuse of "writing a book". Our Bible reading together is a continued source of joy and inspiration. To Craig who discipled me from infancy, reminding me to go to the Bible for the answers. And to those who read the Bible with me, I am grateful for the friendships we enjoy while growing in our understanding of God and His plan for us.

To look into the background for *Point to Reading the Bible*, you can find my first book through Amazon at: *Point to Reading*

Point to Reading: *Hope for the Future Through the Love of Reading*
Second Edition; Copyright © 2013
By Henry Skinner-Larsen   Point to Reading Books

Point to Reading is about the building of relationships between parents and children while reading a fun and engaging book. While you build that close relationship that every parent (and child) desires, your child will receive the added benefit of the love of reading and excellent comprehension skills.

To encourage discipleship and build literacy in Spanish-speaking countries, there is the original Spanish version on Amazon.com:
Apuntar a la Lectura de la Biblia—Mateo 28:20 en Accion

www.ingramcontent.com/pod-product-compliance
Lightning Source LLC
Chambersburg PA
CBHW020955030426
42339CB00005B/114